SpringerBriefs in Health Care Management and Economics

For further volumes:
http://www.springer.com/series/10293

Kristian Wasen
Editor

Emerging
Health Technology

Relocation of Innovative Visual
Knowledge and Expertise

 Springer

Editor
Kristian Wasen
University of Gothenburg
Gothenburg
Sweden

ISSN 2193-1704   ISSN 2193-1712   (electronic)
ISBN 978-3-642-32569-4   ISBN 978-3-642-32570-0   (eBook)
DOI 10.1007/978-3-642-32570-0
Springer Heidelberg New York Dordrecht London

Library of Congress Control Number: 2012949377

© The Author(s) 2013
This work is subject to copyright. All rights are reserved by the Publisher, whether the whole or part of the material is concerned, specifically the rights of translation, reprinting, reuse of illustrations, recitation, broadcasting, reproduction on microfilms or in any other physical way, and transmission or information storage and retrieval, electronic adaptation, computer software, or by similar or dissimilar methodology now known or hereafter developed. Exempted from this legal reservation are brief excerpts in connection with reviews or scholarly analysis or material supplied specifically for the purpose of being entered and executed on a computer system, for exclusive use by the purchaser of the work. Duplication of this publication or parts thereof is permitted only under the provisions of the Copyright Law of the Publisher's location, in its current version, and permission for use must always be obtained from Springer. Permissions for use may be obtained through RightsLink at the Copyright Clearance Center. Violations are liable to prosecution under the respective Copyright Law.
The use of general descriptive names, registered names, trademarks, service marks, etc. in this publication does not imply, even in the absence of a specific statement, that such names are exempt from the relevant protective laws and regulations and therefore free for general use.
While the advice and information in this book are believed to be true and accurate at the date of publication, neither the authors nor the editors nor the publisher can accept any legal responsibility for any errors or omissions that may be made. The publisher makes no warranty, express or implied, with respect to the material contained herein.

Printed on acid-free paper

Springer is part of Springer Science+Business Media (www.springer.com)

Preface

We cannot solve problems by using the same kind of thinking when we created them.

Albert Einstein

Professional health care services that we have become accustomed to are essentially products of technological breakthroughs. Advancements in medicine, such as microwave tomography for breast cancer screening, MRI-guided treatment of prostate cancer and biomedical innovations, such as new 3D, 4D and "5D" in vivo imaging technology, are beginning to facilitate the delivery of reliable tests and rapid diagnostic data. There are several emerging technologies on the horizon.

For example, a recent EU report about the nano-technology roadmap towards 2020 (Joint European Commission, 2009)[1] points to both clinical and economic factors and the beneficial impact of this emerging health technology in regards to diagnostics (e.g., in vivo *imaging* and in vitro *diagnostics*), drug delivery (e.g., *nano-pharmaceuticals* and *nano-devices*), and regenerative medicine (e.g., *cell therapies* and *smart biomaterials*). Emerging *nano-technology applications* are beginning to play a more central role in diagnostics, as they are enabling easier, cheaper, and more sensitive options at the point of care. Thus, medicine is adjusting to the new world of particles at the nano scale, and nano-technologies will become more interesting for health providers as they are cleaner and consume less energy. Nano-technologies, however, require innovative, trans-disciplinary visual knowledge in mixing together different solutions and for them to work efficiently and safely. This fact is underscored in the organisational and human dimension, known as *nano-technique*.[2]

Pharmoeconomics is another emerging research-driven enterprise that pursues ground-breaking work directed towards a new generation of more effective medicines that account for how patients' individually unique genetic compositions affect their responses to medicines. Before the existence of *pharmacogenetics tests*

---

[1] http://www.etp-nanomedicine.eu/public/press-documents/publications/etpn-publications/ 091022_ETPN_Report_2009.pdf   Retrieved May 25 2012

[2] Nano-technique is a term used to describe the human skills involved in executing tasks and facilitating activities on the nano-scale. While nano-technique implies a collection of social and organisational principles, it does not necessarily involve nano-technology but often does.

as modern diagnostic instruments, physicians were restricted in tailoring medications to individual patients' needs and could only make estimates regarding certain symptoms.

Hi-tech innovations have transformed and modernised the entire field of health care delivery with applications ranging from *computerised medical records* and *gene-based diagnostics* to *pharmacy robots* and *image-guided robotic-assisted surgery*.

r-Health = r-Curing and r-Caring

The fact that service robots create new organisational circumstances and novel managerial responsibilities within which new inter-professional and client-expert affairs emerge was something that I pursued in earlier work (Wasen et al. 2002; Wasen 2004). For more than a decade, I have researched and empirically explored the various ways in which health care organisations form, and in turn are formed by, the broad rise of emerging robotic technologies and the new relationships that they create in *r-Curing* and *r-Caring* activities. Some health care fields are experiencing paradigmatic shifts because of robotic technologies, which create entirely new forms of work and interaction among health care staff, which in turn require entirely new professional visual knowledge.

The term r-Curing is used to describe curative treatments that combine the use of robotic technologies with the application of evidence-based medical knowledge. An area in which r-Curing has excelled in medical practice is the use of new *3D, 4D,* and *"5D"*[3] imaging systems in surgery to model and view the patient's body, replacing much of the physical examination and the gentle human touch (see Chap. 2 in this volume). Such state-of-the-art r-Curing systems serve as artificial extensions of the surgeon's body and fundamentally change ancient surgical techniques. The consequence is that humans and their new robotic artefacts become inseparable from each other, i.e., they become *'amalgamated'*. Thus, the well-defined boundary between the individual user and the robotic technology becomes blurred. In the scientific community, the future *human/technology convergence* is increasingly discussed in terms of how *bio-robotics* is empowering human capacity. Bio-robotics provides new treatment options and human capacities; *bionic limbs and exoskeletons* are examples of such emerging health technologies.

---

[3] These visualisation paradigms are specified as follows by Wasen and Brierley in Chap. 2 of this book; "3D imaging is defined as three visual dimensions. 4D imaging is three visual dimensions plus time. 4D imaging can also be combined with functional transitions (i.e., following radioactive tracer isotope through the body in positron emission tomography). 4D imaging plus functionality is defined as "5D" imaging."

r-Caring applications include multi-purpose care-giving robots and how these robots may assist caregivers in their day-to-day work. This trend signifies a move in society towards increased '*self-care*' and patient choice in the elderly care setting, in which elderly patients make shared decisions regarding their treatment options. This development marks an important point of change but also creates new issues in how to organise care delivery. For example, how does the uptake of new "*self-care*" *technologies* and *smart robotic devices* open up the conventional in-house hospital domain and the traditional structures of medical expertise to new, unconventional external and non-clinical markets and patient-grounded work?

While the distinction between health services and care services, or the distinction between professional expertise and patient self-knowledge, are worthwhile considering in understanding how today's elderly care institutions are organised, there will most likely emerge hybrid crossovers in the wider public and private arenas that will link together the two traditionally separate forms of health activities and expertise—*caring* and *curing*.

Self-Organising Nanobots in Nano-Medicine

The modern hospital has become a digitalised "global shop" anchored in a *hybrid cloud-based cyberorganisation*. In future robotic health organisations, most of the electronically mediated communication will be integrated in real-time transmissions of self-generated patient data within cloud-based infrastructures and hybrid networks, which not only will be linked but also pre-analysed in the cloud before they reach a health specialist. The notion of such hybrid smart networks underpins society's characterisation of the future *e-Health* and *m-Health* (Mobile Health) systems, and r-Curing and r-Caring add additional dimensions in what I refer to as the "*new scales of organisation*".

New directions in health robotic technologies are expected to emerge in the coming decades that could take the minimally invasive surgical paradigm and other health care paradigms to a new level: more precisely, to the micro-scale and nano-scale. While nano-manufacturing has taken significant leaps in recent years in different business domains, nano-medicine and nano-biotechnology are new areas to advance the exploration and treatment of the human body. Because of an increased miniaturisation in such medical procedures, and by using the body's natural force (that is, the flow of bodily fluids such as blood), micro-robots and nano-robots equipped with sensor technology will be able to navigate in the human body. These robots would not only navigate but also repair selected organs either automatically or guided by experienced physicians. If the situation allows, these nano-bots would not work alone but in a decentralised fashion in multi-robots teams. Swarms of such tiny robots could cooperate and delegate tasks among themselves. Moreover, these nano-bots could also continually and autonomously supervise the patient's body, for example, to assist damaged organs—thereby monitoring the patients day and night.

Indeed, with the advent of self-organising nano-bots probing layers not visible to the eye, organisational activities will increasingly unfold on the micro-scale and nano-scale. We need to get accustomed to the idea that r-Curing and r-Caring is about emergence of new purposeful forms of work, which function in parallel on different scales of complexity and operability. These new forms of work activities range from nano-bots that self-organise their work and collaboration activities on the nano-scale inside the patient's body, to meso-level activities between entire populations of professionals in hospitals or work carried out in situ between a hospital and a home-based care setting.

It will be imperative to track the broad effects of emerging robotic technologies and new r-Curing and r-Caring services as they are mobilised across the health system. Health care robotics is a novel and exciting technology-enhanced domain at the moment, but it does not solve every problem. We need a combination of solutions.

Why Do We Constantly Need More Pioneering Knowledge?

We need to produce more *innovative knowledge* and deliver more practical solutions in the health care field. Health technology management is a young, cross-disciplinary field. This research aggregates the results and monitors the effects of numerous technological trends, and its multi-layer analysis of in-depth cases allows access to transformative events across different levels within health care systems. A task for scholars is to balance enthusiastic claims for emerging technologies and to place such claims into perspective in the health technology management field. It is vital to remember that health technology is not an end in itself but merely a means to realise the betterment of health and socio-economic prosperity. Providing critical perspectives entails examining how health professionals use technology on their own terms and how they bridge the gap between real-life opportunities and clinical problems involved in managing the complex delivery of health care services.

As technological change is accelerating and affecting the entire health care field, so is professional medical expertise dependent on constantly updating the reservoirs of *visual knowledge*. There is a need to retrain and develop new expertise in many areas of health care following the introduction of new image-guided technologies. For patients as well as health managers and policy makers, professional visual knowledge and medical expertise becomes valuable first if it is made useful and appropriately applied in real-life settings. This book shows that health care processes will improve only if individuals are committed to developing their skills and knowledge; work methods are appropriately changed and thoroughly reconsidered in organisations; and state-of-the-art technologies are entirely incorporated into the hospital or the patient's home environment.

Health professionals are not adequately equipped to solve today's and tomorrow's problems with yesterday's answers and conventional methods. Indeed, because the health care organisation's environment is constantly changing, so too are knowledge, models, and theories in a *temporal* and *fluid state*. Yesterday's best practices and delivery models for highly functioning health care systems may prove to be inadequate to meet today's circumstances and tomorrow's new challenges.

There exist a plentiful amount of great anecdotes of Albert Einstein's life and scientific endeavours. One in particular comes to my mind:

> One day during his tenure as a professor, Albert Einstein was visited by a student. "The questions on this year's exam are the same as last year's!" the young man exclaimed. "Yes," Einstein answered, "but this year all the answers are different".[4]

While many fundamental questions and concerns remain in the health care field, the answers have clearly changed, not least because of the impact of rapid technological change in business and society. The message is quite simple; we constantly need more innovative knowledge driven by creative processes of *serendipity*.

Change Management in Health Care: Novel Technology, New Organisation?

Change management seeks an orderly transition towards new modes of process change in health delivery and, more generally, organisational renewal. Change management therefore necessitates carefully considered, mindfully integrated, and meticulously calibrated measures and plans that fit into the broader organisational structures and professional cultures. Any emerging technological innovation will inevitably lead to transformations in most or all of the work tasks situated at an organisational level, among professionals collaborating at a group level, and at an individual level within a doctor's interactions with a patient. Regarding change-management initiatives, it is vital to remember that technology is not the universal solution for improving health care processes. However, emerging health technologies will continue to be vital enablers of many innovative knowledge-driven, process-change initiatives.

Clearly, not all long-standing institutional, economical and social problems can be solved by merely adding new technical fixes and technological devices. Exploring the emergence of today and tomorrow's prevalent *health care management* dilemmas and challenges (demographical, organisational, managerial, technological, medical, political, etc.) will inevitably entail cross-disciplinary research which, in turn, includes a wider and deeper spectrum of viewpoints to find more safe, efficient, and economically viable solutions. The need to embrace

---

[4] "Albert Einstein Anecdotes—The Gold Scales" http://oaks.nvg.org/sa5ra17.html Retrieved May 25 2012.

the challenges and benefits of emerging health technologies goes hand-in-hand with the need to transform the present institutional structures of health care delivery and to rethink traditional patient–doctor relationships. To fully optimise the use of any technological device, the first step is to understand that novel health technologies allow new forms of work in treating patients, and they create new spaces of curing and caring. In short, health technologies enable new *social* and *material relationships*. However, exchanging antiquated technologies for modern ones almost always means changing work processes and the conventional knowledge and expertise that are required to carry out old tasks with old technologies. In other words, adapting to more advanced and complex technologies requires more-advanced, knowledge-intensive services in health care. Adapting to new technologies also requires that the end-users accept them (rather than resist them) and demonstrate a willingness to engage in training programme so that they better can understand both the new work tasks and the technologies.

Who Is This Book For?

This book compiles a variety of viewpoints on transformative technological change and its limits in health care institutions. These viewpoints are theoretically informed and empirically based, and the authors tackle some of the most pressing issues health professionals face today. Moreover, the book comprises diverse and cross-disciplinary contributions, ranging from organisational behaviour and change/innovation management literatures to theories in science, technology and society and models of technology acceptance. The book is intended for scholars in the cross-disciplinary field of *health technology management*. This book is also a useful resource for students in graduate and postgraduate programs, including the Master's program in Health Management and Public Health (MBA/MPH).

This volume contains chapters that report cutting-edge cases of emerging health technologies. This book seeks to explore emerging health care technologies such as image-guided surgical robotics, pharmacy robots, visualisation methods (3D, 4D & "5D") and home telehealth management systems and their acceptance in the workplace but also, more generally, their special role in business and society. The book describes the emerging relocation of innovative knowledge and expertise within health care organisations and beyond, such as in the patient's home environment. The relocation of certain knowledge areas from physicians to patients in self-care management or the reconfiguration of health care expertise from one health profession to another are examples of topics developed in this book.

Here, as I see it, r-Health, m-Health and e-Health services can have a significant impact on the manner in which health care delivery models are implemented through cost-saving frameworks. Health technologies are increasingly being used, for example, in robotic-based (r-Health) applications (Chaps. 2 and 3) and in teleconsultation in e-Health and m-Health applications either between physicians or between patients and doctors (Chaps. 4 and 5). These technologies allow health care professionals to effectively reach far beyond the current service offerings, providing new methods for communication, diagnosis, and treatment.

In the years ahead, there will be an increasing amount of preventive self-care initiatives and associated devises that inform patients of their health conditions (see Chaps. 4 and 5 in this volume). in this volume). Some of the authors in this volume focus on disruptive, game-changing health technologies that are reforming the practice of health care. Teleconsultation and homecare, for example, result in less travel time for both patients and medical practitioners. Hence, today's health care providers need to prepare increasingly technologically savvy citizens, who can perform an increasing number of diagnostic tasks using innovative self-care technologies in their home environments. Clearly, emerging health technologies are a cornerstone of tomorrow's efforts to address these challenges. The emerging technologies offer health care institutions and management new systems for delivering health care services.

Acknowledgments

I would like to thank all of the contributors of this book for their commitment and effort in rethinking today's emerging health technologies and tomorrow's organisation, delivery and rearrangement of health care practices. The idea to realise this book project was born while I was a visiting scholar and postdoctoral fellow in Canada. So, I would like to thank all of my Canadian colleagues who provided interesting comments and thoughtful suggestions during my talks and seminars at the University of Calgary.

I would also like to thank my colleagues Mary Jo Hatch and Jill Woodilla, two prominent scholars in business studies and management science, who were generous with their time to read and critique my texts. Thank you so much for your support and encouragement. In the final stage of this book project, Aant Elzinga at the University of Gothenburg brought his extensive expertise and experience in the field of Science and Technology Studies (STS) to provide valuable comments and constructive critics on the final drafts, and I truly appreciate his help.

The contribution in Chap. 4 appeared in *International Journal of Medical Informatics* published by Elsevier. Permission from Elsevier Science to republish the article is gratefully acknowledged. The publication of this book has been possible thanks to the financial support of the Jan Wallander and Tom Hedelius Foundation and of the Swedish Council for Working Life and Social Research.

Gothenburg, Sweden   Kristian Wasen

Contents

1 Introduction
   Kristian Wasen   1

2 The Visual Touch Regime: Real-Time 3D Image-Guided
   Robotic Surgery and 4D and "5D" Scientific Illustration at Work
   Kristian Wasen and Meaghan Brierley   21

3 New Technologies in British Pharmacy Practice
   Kimberly Jamie.   53

4 Patients' Perceptions of a Home Telecare System
   Mohammadreza Rahimpour, Nigel H. Lovell,
   Branko G. Celler and John McCormick   75

5 A Framework for Future Studies of Personalised Medicine:
   Affordance, Travelling, and Governance of Expertise
   Morten Sager, Fredrik Bragesjö and Aant Elzinga   101

Contributors

Fredrik Bragesjö University of Gothenburg, Gothenburg, Sweden

Meaghan Brierley University of Calgary, Calgary, AB, Canada

Branko G. Celler University of New South Wales, Sydney, Australia

Aant Elzinga University of Gothenburg, Gothenburg, Sweden

Kimberly Jamie University of York, York, UK

Nigel H. Lovell University of New South Wales, Sydney, Australia

John McCormick University of New South Wales, Sydney, Australia

Mohammadreza Rahimpour University of New South Wales, Sydney, Australia

Morten Sager University of Gothenburg, Gothenburg, Sweden

Kristian Wasen University of Gothenburg, Gothenburg, Sweden

Chapter 1
Introduction

Kristian Wasen

Abstract The opening chapter addresses the different ways in which visual knowledge and medical health expertise are being reorganised and relocated and thereby reinforced and disputed in new practices of professional work involving state-of-the-art health technology. Change management and related concepts are discussed and defined. The chapter shows that emerging health technologies, organisational renewal, and the discovery of unexpected innovative knowledge are highly interconnected in professional practice. Emerging health technology refers both to new work, physical devices, and visual knowledge and expertise that, when located and relocated in the institutional landscape—or combined and recombined in health practices—may unfold unexpectedly into new patient-doctor constellations and organisational structures.

Keywords Health technology management • Change management • Organisational innovation • Serendipity and creativity • 3D/4D/"5D" visualisation and imaging technology • Cloud computing in health care

1.1 Socio-Economic and Demographic Trends

It is no coincidence that the delivery structure of health care services is under continuous public scrutiny and a topic of controversies and debates. As Groll et al. (2002) note in their editorial in the *British Medical Journal (BMJ)*, "Headlines in newspapers, statements in policy documents, and many analyses, surveys and reports repeatedly highlight serious problems in health care delivery related to underuse, overuse, or misuse of care." (2002, p. 110) Indeed, because health care has such a central role in people's lives, for a modern state and its citizen, functioning and accessible health care services not only entail existential security and the enhancement of aging people's quality of life. On occasion, they more

K. Wasen (✉)
University of Gothenburg, Gothenburg, Sweden
e-mail: kristian.wasen@gu.se

drastically imply the difference between life and death, for oneself, a family member or a friend.

Indeed, it is possible to argue that the increased (or reduced) accessibility to additional premium health care services is intertwined with citizens' understanding of the level of wealth and prosperity in society. From the citizens' and customers' point of view, new medical knowledge and health expertise, in concert with the employment of emerging technologies, may help to cure the incurable, and in doing so, emerging technologies as well as certain medical knowledge leaps raise the public's expectations of continuous improvements in the health care sector.

How do we expect health care delivery to change in the coming decades, taking into consideration the demographic trends in many countries around the world? The average life expectancy has increased in many countries and will continue to do so. Most of us agree that it is encouraging that people can survive more deadly deceases, stay healthy and live longer. According to the UN's (United Nations) current forecasts, the global population growth is expected to reach somewhere between 7.5 and 10 billion by 2050, meaning that more people will need food, fresh water, a good education, and access to health care. The global population growth in the years ahead will most likely place additional pressure on health systems, particularly in countries lacking well-developed health care infrastructures. Health and wealth are closely interrelated.

According to recent data from the Organization for Economic Cooperation and Development (OECD),[1] health care spending continues to surpass economic growth in the majority of the OECD countries:

> Health spending continues to rise faster than economic growth in most OECD countries, maintaining a trend observed since the 1970s. Health spending reached 9.5 % of GDP on average in 2009, the most recent year for which figures are available, up from 8.8 % in 2008, according to OECD Health Data 2011. But health spending as a share of GDP is likely to stabilise or fall slightly in 2011. This is due to improving economic growth and lower health spending.

Clearly, as stated by the OECD, health care institutions will be addressing multifaceted transformations in various forms, and when faced with limited resources, many governments (and health care providers) will do their best to keep costs down as they seek to rein in budget deficits. The OECD interestingly concludes that "[w]hile governments must do more to get better value for money from health care spending, they must also continue pursuing their long-term goals of having more equitable, responsive and efficient health systems."

How do we expect health care delivery to change in the coming decades, taking into consideration significant challenges in the institutional landscape? Different countries are clearly choosing different health care strategies and delivery models to meet their demand for high quality and affordable care. Most health care institutions are under pressure and need to solve upcoming issues and rapidly

---

[1] OECD newsroom "Health: Spending continues to outpace economic growth in most OECD countries" http://www.oecd.org/ Retrieved May 28, 2012.

transform themselves to maintain the quality of health services while simultaneously lowering costs. According to the OECD (2005) report "Health Technologies and Decision Making," technological change is commonly considered the main source of rising health care expenditures. Indeed, cost containment seems to have become the *sine qua non strategy* to counteract rising health care expenditures and to achieve high quality and affordable care. If cost-efficiency programs are successfully implemented, existing resources can be used more optimally, thus enabling additional premium health care services and treatments for more citizens.

Various improvement programs initiated by health management executives can only be successfully implemented if they are interlinked with organisational change initiatives. Thus, the management of a health care system and its institutions is not merely confined to complex administrative decision-making and economic matters. A key problem is that new technologies are implemented within antiquated organisational structures. The efficient uptake of new health technology requires equivalent nimble, innovative, and adjustable organisational changes.

1.2 Theory and Practice of Change Management

The science of change management and organisational development is not new (see e.g., Leavitt 1965; Burnes 2004; Greener and Hughes 2006; Marshak 2005; Heimer Rathbone 2012), but it is increasingly being applied in the health care domain. Formalised change management initiatives were established in the business domain, and several commonly used definitions still primarily refer to corporate settings and business practices. According to the Collins English Dictionary (2010), *change management* is "a style of management that aims to encourage organizations and individuals to deal effectively with the changes taking place in their work". Moreover, the SHRM Glossary of Human Resources Terms characterises it as "[t]he systematic approach and application of knowledge, tools and resources to deal with change. Change management means defining and adopting corporate strategies, structures, procedures and technologies to deal with changes in external conditions and the business environment". (Tracey 2003).

The topic of change is not in itself a new topic either in management studies (it was theorised in the beginning) or in other social sciences such as sociology. However, cross-disciplinary research that extends the traditional viewpoints on change dilemmas is of great value and should be encouraged. Science and Technology Studies (STS) is helpful precisely because it provides a critical lens on the materialities that are involved in organisational processes. STS research has theorised and placed a greater emphasis on how technological projects are regulated, re-configured and how new social relationships are made possible. Hence while similar notions of change management have emerged within other social science disciplines, they have taken a somewhat different direction.

Management science increasingly has showed an appreciation for the unravelling ambiguities and uncertainties that are prevalent in contemporary work practices (Tsoukas and Chia 2002), which can potentially disorganise and destabilise traditional divisions of labour. In this chapter, the notions of change and continuity, or transformation and stability, are not seen as mutually exclusive but rather as co-existing in different fashions and constellations.

In recent years, several scholars in management studies and organisation theory have turned to the philosophical work of postmodernist thinkers Deleuze and Guattari (2004) to discuss the immanent dynamic unfolding changes and transformational qualities that are to be found in contemporary institutional settings (e.g., Boje 2006; Linstead and Thanem 2007; Styhre 2005, Sørensen 2005).

Deleuze and Guattari's notion of *assemblage* is appealing because it overcomes the dualistic relationships between change and stability, form and substance, subjects and objects, the Cartesian dichotomy between mind and body, or other aspects of life that are reduced to either/or relationships. Styhre (2010a) emphasises that assemblage is not merely a philosophical term to be theoretically examined but that it should be scrutinised and observed in empirical settings. Such an approach entails exploring the concept, thus: "… sociomaterial practices are to be examined qua practices, practical undertakings, rather than being a set of propositions of conjecture" (Styhre, 2010a, p. 65). The term assemblage highlights functional productive relationships, and it is "… the process of arranging, organizing, and fitting together a multiplicity of heterogeneous elements into a consistent, vibrant and functional entity that primarily serves the role of productive means, just like an abstract machine…" (Livesey 2005, p. 18–19).

Assemblages, Livesey continues,

> … are complex constellations of objects, bodies, expressions, qualities, and territories that come together for varying periods of time to ideally create new ways of functioning /… / An assemblage emerges when a function emerges; ideally it is innovative and productive. The result of a productive assemblage is a new means of expression, a new territorial/spatial organization, a new institution, a new behavior, or a new realization. The assemblage is destined to produce a new reality, by making numerous, often unexpected, connections (ibid, p. 19).

Hence, change is always immanent in a space and territory. As I demonstrate later on in this chapter, in image-guided robotic practices, for example, surgeons are suddenly seeing things they did not perceive before in traditional open surgery. Thus their new visual environment represents a new function. The manifestation of such a particular assemblage includes a new means of visual expression in which new innovative knowledge about patients' bodies is created. High-end optical devices not only create a particular way of seeing and perceiving anatomy through multidimensional (3D, 4D, "5D") imaging technology but also create a new territorial/spatial organisation (see quote above), i.e. a particular way to organise visual records and work activities in operating theatres.

I return to the question of change and new territorial spaces, and I will argue in the chapter that we need to assess both the *stabilities* (organisation) and *instabilities* (disorganisation) to understand how the employment of emerging technologies spatially relocates visual knowledge and medical expertise in practice.

Clearly, change management has extended beyond its traditional prevalence in corporate settings into health care management settings (e.g. Groll et al. 2002; McNulty and Ferlie 2002; Roback 2006; Van de Ven 1991). Examining and studying organisational change as it unfolds in situ in the workplace does not only mean embracing new innovative devices, but more importantly, it also means observing how new innovative thinking and novel knowledge is produced to improve the organisation and its processes (cf. Lave and Wenger 1991). The implementation of new health technology applications is an organisational challenge and involves a responsive governance and constant adjustments. While the quality improvement of health care is a declared objective among health service providers worldwide at present, safe, reliable, and effective delivery is not always obvious: "Health systems are sometimes unsafe and frequently we harm patients who have trusted us with their care. There is an endemic failure to engage patients with decisions about their care. We know there are problems; we just need to change so that care can be made safer and better." (Groll et al. 2002, p. 110).

What is more, change management, despite being well-intentioned, may quickly become risk management, or even worse, crisis management. No matter how sophisticated the novel technology may be and no matter how heedful and proactive the health care management is, there is no point in making major investments in technology if the health practitioners and/or patients are not on board and ready to embrace the very technology in question. All parties should be able to utilise the technology efficiently in everyday practice. Stakeholder involvement, support and acceptance cannot be underestimated in any organisational-technological transformation in health care. Health technology will be unsuccessful or unproductive if its end-users do not feel comfortable using it.

To avoid a situation in which expensive sophisticated medical devices are sitting idle in a closet, there must first exist a state of what some scholars and practitioners refer to as "organisational readiness" or "organisational adjustment". Such reactive organisations are more prone to rapidly and successfully adjust in response to the challenges posed by emerging health technologies. Interestingly, the California Telemedicine and eHealth Institute[2] describes organisational readiness as a mind-set and as "the ability and willingness of an organisation to shift from its current way of operating". A health care institution's management regulation should encourage such willingness, adaptability and organisational readiness. These are key factors in being prepared to embrace the benefits and address the drawbacks of any emerging medical technology.

---

[2] www.cteconline.org/general-information/organizational-readiness-guide "Assessing organizational readiness" Retrieved May 28, 2012.

1.3 What is Emerging in Emerging Health Technology?

My understanding of the word *emergence*[3] refers to something new and implies changes that result in unplanned events and effects. While some refinements are more or less known and produce expected results, most "emerging" events appear and materialise unexpectedly. Drawing on this general idea, I will use the verb 'emerging' to refer to (A) a more complex technological device (B) a process of transformative change in the way a health care activity (e.g., a work task) is carried out, and finally (C) a specific process in creating new discontinuous visual knowledge and innovations. There exist other meanings of 'emergence' than the three provided here.

One additional and important dimension is that technologies not only emerge but also unexpectedly re-emerge. The erratic effects of emerging technology partly lie in its proliferation into new and unexpected domains of application. This idea is supported by studies of large-scale changes in society, which have found that most advanced and complex emerging technologies are in fact multifaceted rather than single-purposed. Adner and Levinthal (2002), for example, maintain that many significant shifts in society occur because a known technology is being innovatively re-reconfigured in a completely novel domain of usage. "Seeming revolutions such as wireless communication and the Internet did not stem from an isolated technical breakthrough; rather, their spectacular commercial impact was achieved when an existing technology was re-applied in a new application domain" (Adner and Levinthal 2002, p. 45). In a similar line of reasoning, Simon (1987) claims that key enabling technologies in the Industrial Revolution were not deployed for a single purpose but rather created opportunities for a series of refined inventions in different areas and applications. In fact, all of these examples support the general idea that technology "re-emerges" unexpectedly and is relocated from one domain into new application domains.

Few would deny the significance of technology in contemporary economies and societies. Harvey Brooks, a former Dean of the Harvard University School of Applied Physics, argues that the body of knowledge that professionals must utilise and the rising societal expectations of professionals are tightly coupled with rapid technological change: "The problem cannot be usefully phrased in terms of too

---

[3] The origin of the word emergence derives from the Latin *'emergere'* ('become known', 'brought to light') (Concise Oxford English Dictionary 2011). However, in modern language, the term 'emergence' has various meanings attached to it, and the notion of "coming into being" is rather limited. All three meanings that I ascribe to the word 'emerging' suggest that something is changing into a more advanced and complex state. However, simply because technology is emerging unexpectedly, it does not necessarily develop into a better or an absolute ideal state. Fridlund (1999) points out that 'development' can be a problematic concept, as it is based on the assumption in natural science that species evolve into a higher form in biological evolution. Likewise, in the history of science, management science and other social sciences, a similar (implicit) assumption is that social or managerial systems evolve to a higher and ultimately superior state in the process of a corporate, historical or societal evolution.

much technology. Rather it is whether we can generate technological change fast enough to meet the expectations and demands that technology itself has generated" (1967, p. 89).

Brooks draws attention here to a rapidly changing technological environment in which professionals need to embrace a higher degree of adaptability and rate of knowledge acquisition. However, as I will demonstrate, technology is as much about devices as about knowledge. In fact, the fundamental connotations of knowledge are deeply entwined with the conceptual distinction between *technology* and *technique*.

The word technique usually refers to a collection of principles and human endeavours being developed over a period of time in which experience and mastery are gained through continuous training and practice. (cf. Ericsson et al. 2007) Technique does not necessarily involve the word technology, but in many instances, it does so because technology in everyday usage refers to the actual application of the technique and the specific devices and tools that enhance the efficiency of the factual technique. In Western academia, the scholarly usage of the term *technology* is not merely confined to physical instruments and machines but rather includes the multitude of human skills, processes and activities that are required for operating complex systems. Technology is regarded as "knowledge-enhanced meanings of doing something practical with tools" (Hatch 2011, p. 40). Technology, more generally, thus refers to physical devices as well as human knowledge and expertise that, when combined and recombined, are necessary to develop and employ tools, equipment, and work methods that produce a certain service or product. This extended meaning of technology is also reflected in a conceptual delineation of the term "medical technology" provided by the Office of Technology Assessment (Office of Technology Assessment 1976, p. 86), which defines technology,

.... as 'science or knowledge applied to a definite purpose'. Thus, medical technology includes all elements of medical practice that are knowledge-based, including hardware (e.g., equipment and facilities) and software (e.g., knowledge and skills). Medical technology is defined as the set of techniques, drugs, equipment, and procedures used by healthcare professionals in delivering medical care to individuals and the systems within which such care is delivered.

Clearly, technology has various connotations in different scientific fields. Not surprisingly, the pragmatic and conceptual roots for viewing technology as a means of achieving results are found in economics and management science. Moreover, the conceptual roots are also found in other disciplines, such as economic history, anthropology, and sociology. In organisational theory, the corporate enterprise is sometimes conceptualised and understood more broadly as a technology in itself that produces certain goods and services for the benefit of society (Hatch 1997). Other viewpoints on technology conceptualise it as a key internal element of the organisation, a perspective that places an emphasis on the work carried out in transforming inputs to outputs. (Leavitt 1965).

There exist as many different definitions of technology as there are definitions of *organisations*. Conventionally, the basic understanding of the term *organisation* is that it is a social system that consists of two or more people who carry out tasks to fulfil a set goal. Some scholars have argued that technology should be conceptualised on symmetrical terms with human workers, thus describing human and "non-human" actors. However, more recent research has demonstrated that technology is used and perceived as *"surrogate co-workers"* (e.g., Wasen 2010) having both social and functional abilities. Accordingly, this definition expands the traditional notions of organisation and socio-technical systems, in that organisations are social and asocial (functional) structures wherein material and non-material dimensions interplay. Thus, if two robots carry out a common task or if a human worker delegates a dangerous, monotonous or tiresome task to a robotic "co-worker," an organisation is formed insofar as an established goal is fulfilled.

1.4 Real-Time Relocation of Health Expertise

In a sociological critique of the powerful reciprocity between the technological and the social aspects of health care, Webster (2007) argues that emerging health technologies open the opportunity for new social relationships, the creation of new disease groupings, and new categories of patients. Technology may challenge lay/expert relations upon which we have depended, such as the professional–patient relationships found in conventional medical practice. The standardised professional knowledge upon which these social relationships depend may become weakened and contestable. (Webster 2007).

Thus, to understand how present health care provision models are changing and being challenged by new emerging health technologies, it becomes imperative to understand how professional health care expertise and physical work tasks are reorganised and relocated in new ways.

Hatch (2011) succinctly notes that organising requires coordinated efforts to accomplish desired future states and that"… regardless of the technology they use, employees are affected by the distribution and arrangement of the spaces they occupy, so designing physical spaces to support technology promotes efficiency and effectiveness" (Hatch 2011, p. 39). More generally, when coordinated work activities are moved to new locations, institutionally based knowledge and human expertise also move to form new arrangements of spaces. Consequently, by real-time relocation we mean a spatial movement of material and immaterial resources taking place simultaneously in several organisational contexts.[4] An effect of such a

---

[4] Relocation is an important term in business practices and in management studies. The term is perhaps most notably used within inter-organisational collaborations and M&As (Mergers and Acquisitions). (see e.g., Baaij et al. 2004; Wasen 2005a, b) The latter are corporate transformations in which two or more organisations unite into a single enterprise. In M&As and other complex reorganisations, managers not only search for ways to promote efficiency and effectiveness through cost savings and taking measures to minimise the administrative overhead but also by rearranging the locations of professionals and their expertise in new, more efficient constellations. For example, employees move to a new location or a firm establishes an office or a production facility in a new location.

relocation is that the knowledge that was previously distributed in one way becomes re-distributed in new ways, often mediated through new technologies or, more recently, embedded within the technology itself.

1.4.1 Hybrid Cloud-Based Work Environments: Virtual or Material?

Clearly, the outreach of human expertise and medical knowledge in health care is currently extended along broader geographical areas and mediated in real-time through the Internet and emerging smart-cloud applications.

While the patient is increasingly transformed into a manageable "digital unit", health care still addresses the treatment of human bodies that are bound to spatial contexts and material situations.[5] Indisputably, the 'virtual turn' in institutional life has important applications in the health care domain, for example, in allowing surgeons to develop their skills and operate on 'virtual bodies' in simulator environments instead of training on living patients. However, it is unfortunate when proponents of the 'virtual' context suggest that modern work and the allocation of resources in institutional settings no longer is dependent on a firm's (and its employees') physical location, instead arguing that such distribution is situated in "fluid" information-based virtual structures. They disregard how materiality and spatiality influence and shape human relationships and play a key role in the relocation and redistribution of human expertise, work activities and relationships. Hybrid cloud-based work environments are both virtual and material.

Interestingly and unexpectedly, emerging health technologies in such work environments can redefine and reorganise, and perhaps sometimes disorganise, existing patient-doctor relationships found in the hospital ward and beyond. As some of the contributions in this present volume suggest, the relocation of human boundaries and relationships regularly entail shifts in epistemic boundaries. Hence, while emerging health technologies in many cases involve physical relocation as they both shape and reshape the practices and "spatialities of care" (Schillmeier and Domènech 2010), they also cause imperative changes in the distribution of work and alter the prevailing stock of medical knowledge.

The augmented mobility of information resources and the virtual distribution of knowledge and expertise still heavily depend on spatial and material infrastructures to function properly. Consequently, reorganisation and relocation activities are not merely confined to 'the virtual' and 'the digital' but also to the spatial,

---

[5] The various forms of virtual management tools and portals have gained increasing popularity not just in health care but in the business world in general. This trend is to a certain extent inspired by the vast transformations that took place in virtual banking over the last decades. The economic mobility entailed the real-time flow of monetary resources in digitally based commodity trading and the instantaneous access to and transfer of money. Virtual banking flows are also mediated through unified ICT-based financial networks on a global scale.

material dimensions of existing health care practices (for example, see Chaps. 2 and 5 in this volume).

1.4.2 Toward Optimised and Economically Viable Self-Care Services

Debates on the future organisation of health care are parts of broader discussions on the nature of technological change. Such discussions are increasingly concerned with the attractiveness and cost-efficiency of new medical technologies that allow for dislocated remote treatments that are at times executed by the patients themselves. There is a trend towards the increased usage of a variety of self-care services (i.e., "self-management" devices). In the present proliferation of health care technologies ranging from eHealth to mHealth applications, optimisation, safety and efficiency have been identified as key factors for success. As these networks span local, regional and national borders, we might actually think about health services being delivered in trans-regional or trans-national health networks. The hospital has become a digitalised "global shop" anchored in a hybrid cloud-based cyberorganisation.

Facing new challenges in a cloud-based data management environment, there is more to safe operations than reliable technologies and detailed procedures. Daniels (2011, p. 1 and 9) notes that:

> Organizations are increasing initiatives in cloud computing driven by simplicity, affordability, and sustainability factors, but remain cautious with implementations as security risks are evaluated and analyzed /.../ Cloud computing offers increasingly flexible methods of system integration. Hot failovers, highly available systems, real-time relocation of virtual systems, dynamic reallocation of system resources, and even wide-area network disaster recovery (backup) are features of the virtualized cloud computing environment.

Real-time data management in emerging cloud-based systems allows real-time storage, and users can procure information that is current. The agility of information exchange means that data and expertise move and flow in fast rhythms between the network nodes that can be groups of physicians, individual patients, large databases, health care institutions, or automated machines—from one hospital to another, from one patient to his/her doctor, or from a heart rate sensor coupled to a self-care medical device. This device may allow the patient to stay home because it is located at the bedside in the patient's residence, but the device is directly connected to a cloud-based service and transfers patient data continuously to a remote doctor in a hospital on the other side of the globe. Such institutional infrastructures of emerging cloud-based health services depend on security strategies for privacy protection (Daniels 2011; Pearson and Charlesworth 2009) and a "fail-safe" technological infrastructure that continuously interfaces between people and organisations.

How do we know if a complex technological system in a health care setting is sufficiently reliable? Put in simple terms, health care services and digital asset activities should flow smoothly and predictability throughout the network. However, Edwards (2010) notes that when large amounts of data travel between different machines and computer systems in the context of large database infrastructures, such a transfer is not always consistent, and data can also be distorted and misapprehended, leading to what Edwards terms "data friction". Data frictions can occur in mHealth services. Therefore, emerging forms of health care jobs and provisions of new mHealth services will require tailored institutional arrangements, both strategically and operationally, to manage data friction. The latter means that safety is achieved in the day-to-day activities because a nurse's job, for example, may be directly dependent on the patient carrying out certain procedures in due time. If frictions or delays occur in this interplay, then the nurse cannot do his/her job, thereby creating a less optimised system. Hence, new types of work arrangements in mHealth must be institutionally consistent, just as tools and machines that are used as intermediaries between patients and care givers must be reliable. Technological expertise is required to optimise the implementation of machines in local settings and adjusted to local needs, but safety also extends from pure reliable machine knowledge to matters of institutional work design, logistics and cost-effectiveness.

In other words, when we think of how to promote optimal and competitive solutions, entire networks should be considered to achieve the successful uptake of mHealth technologies. These technologies are becoming increasingly sophisticated, automated and flexible but still require human expertise and appropriately modified social interactions to function efficiently. The successful integration of people and health care technologies requires new knowledge to be developed and applied. As services allow some self-care work tasks to be performed by patients themselves, knowledge and skills may be transferred from physicians to patients (clients) as well. We can actually see this happen now because the mHealth trend is indicative of a shift in the distribution of medical knowledge and the allocation of expertise in the health system. Patients are becoming increasingly involved in individualised treatments, and they develop knowledge that only physicians previously acquired. The patients execute some of the tasks that physicians previously did.

Hence, eHealth, mHealth and rHealth brings cyberinteractions to the forefront (see Preface in this volume). In principle, not only physician-patient consultations as we know in eHealth but more complex medical treatments (such as remote patient-doctor consultations) can be carried out at a distance, leading to entirely new perspectives and more efficient health care services. Many patients would like to have this capability to engage in mHealth. Many health care managers and funders of health care would prefer such solutions, as they believe these treatments may increase efficiencies and lower costs at a time when economies are strained.

Cost-effective and cost-saving solutions, whereby patients accomplish more of the work themselves with the assistance of automated and smart machines, are therefore attractive in publicly funded health care and elderly care systems and in private insurance-based regimes. A current institutional strategy is to distribute health care services across various geographical areas, across time, and across a variety of health care technologies. The implications that this arrangement will have, especially the role that emerging health technologies will play, are the focus of the following section.

1.5 Image-Guided Medicine: Toward a New Distribution of Work

Sociologists Berger and Luckmann (1967) pinpoint the dynamic distribution of human expertise in a society, which renders certain specialised roles and distribution of labour possible. Indeed, most emerging image-guided health technologies entail new ways of doing work and novel ways of seeing and carrying out habitual tasks, thus providing new types of information, knowledge, and techniques that can be used to diagnose diseases that were previously untreatable. In this chapter, I have maintained that emerging health technology is as much about innovative visual knowledge as about devices and gadgets. As Styhre (2010b) notes, visual practices may play a key role in organisational settings:

> Professional vision thus includes aesthetic judgment but also includes other qualities such the economic aspect of the modus operandi, i.e., the ability to undertake a practice in an effective and skilled manner. Professional vision not only examines the outcomes but constitutes the very procedures for producing such output/.../Taken together, vision and visuality in organizations may play a more central role in forthcoming regimes of economic production; professional vision as the integration and embodiment of a series of professional skills and capacities is therefore a highly relevant concept that is applicable in a variety of domains, fields, and industries, all obeying their own instituted beliefs, values, norms, and practices. (Styhre 2010b, p. 176–177)

Professional vision is domain-specific in the field of health care and diagnostics, and some professional experts are more likely to diagnose a disease correctly than others. For Rystedt et al. (2011, p. 765), expertise "… is not simply a matter of providing correct explanations, but also involves discovery work in which visual renderings are made transparent". The radiology profession, for example, primarily relies on digital representations of the patient's body rather than physical touch as surgeons do.

Mondada's (2003) study focuses on a laparoscopic team's accomplishment of knowledge-based collaborative physical tasks and the ways in which medical images are being produced, used, and interpreted in the surgical workplace. It considers the visual skills and expertise required to see with a camera that involves particular ways of seeing, acting, and knowing. Mondada shows how the presentation of small-scale anatomical details on television screens can be used as a powerful conversational resource in collaborative surgical tasks. Linguistic cues (both verbal and non-verbal) in the professional practice of an operating room are required to identify and initiate actions required of other team members. Such cues are also used to confirm that actions have been correctly executed in the operating room (OR). By utilising 2D imaging camera systems in laparoscopic surgery, the surgical team maintains task awareness and achieves a common ground and understanding. This process is a type of mentoring collaborative task in which the assistant surgeon is guided by the lead surgeon's direction. (Mondada 2003).

Both radiological and surgical expertise involve situated and embodied reasoning. (Rystedt et al. 2011; Mondada 2003) Whereas physicians have traditionally relied on their natural sight in their direct interaction with organs and pathological objects, they now increasingly rely on new 3D and 4D imaging techniques (see Chap. 2 this volume). The surgeons literally see the anatomy when the 4D dataset has been colour coded in 3D, and surgeons can touch virtual tissues and almost have the feeling that they are inside of the tissue. This emerging imaging technology provides the clinician with a much more natural way to work with 3D and 4D data because merely looking at a 2D screen and a slice of the thumb is not a natural way to examine the data and to appreciate the thumb's 3D structure. It is more effective if the surgeons can see a 3D structure in front them and interact with it by rotating and feeling it. Technology offers new possibilities and enhances the experts' ability to interact with that data and to understand the real 3D structure.

Moreover, when physicians are beginning to apply new health technologies, such as new 3D and 4D imaging systems, in surgery, these surgical professionals are involved in complex improvement work to discover new, innovative medical knowledge in vivo. In my perspective, the practices of seeing and knowing in multi-sensorial worlds (3D, 4D, "5D"), for example, are coupled with the creative *processes of serendipity* in medical and scientific knowledge. *Serendipity* can be an ordinary experience—a "pleasant surprise"—for professionals, but it can also be more of an astonishing Wow "Aha" experience. Targama and Wasen (2005, p. 80) note that the latter may trigger a reconsideration of an individual's understanding: "What happens in the social interaction process is that people get stimuli that trigger an individual process of questioning and assessing their own understanding".

In a study of an established visualisation practices in radiology, Rysted et al. (2011) describe the professional rearrangement of work following the implementation of tomosynthesis, a new advanced imaging technology. The expanded technological environment in radiology work implied that the staff needed "… to calibrate their methods, interpretations, and understandings with respect to a novel technology" (Rystedt et al. 2011, p. 886). To confirm or contest observations among experts, for example, in identifying a tumour, new technology had to be used in parallel with the older computed tomography (CT). The so called "clinical gaze" may shift (Foucault 1973). In so doing, the human use of technology changes the role of clinical judgment, and ultimately the power of expert knowledge that medical specialists have benefitted from in society (Webster 2007).

The current relocation of certain knowledge areas from physicians to patients in home-based self-care management or the reconfiguration of health care expertise from one health profession to another are examples of themes developed and scrutinised in this volume. This book on emerging health technologies addresses a variety of themes on innovative visual knowledge and the relocation of expertise.

1.6 Outline of the Book

The chapters by *Kristian Wasen* and *Meaghan Brierley* and by *Kimberly Jamie* both draw attention to the organisational and technological attributes involved in the relocation of expertise and knowledge in so called *r-Health* (Robotic Health) *practices* (see the Preface, this volume).

In Chap. 2, *Kristian Wasen* and *Meaghan Brierley* consider the emerging visual touch regimes and the professional reorganisation of interactions, skills and expertise to see and touch in real-time multidimensional imaging (3D, 4D, "5D"). The shift from old regimes, such as laparoscopic surgery, to new regimes of work implies the end of existing organisational practices in favour of newer, more effective ones that add value to the health care system. Professionals' adjustment to new health care technologies and the acceptance of new practices represent a point of institutional innovation.

The organisational transformation involves a transition from the use of knowledge and expertise founded on tactile feedback in traditional work to a dependence on visual knowledge and expertise in image-guided robotic practices. The authors empirically show how modern health technology mediations fundamentally reconfigure and reshape the meaning and uses of the terms digital vision and digital touch in professional practices of robotic surgery and scientific illustration.

The chapter develops the idea of the emerging visual-touch regime, a notion that draws on the significant difference between "touching with the hand" and *"touching with the eye"*. The latter represents a new form of knowledge work. Moreover, the latter stands in contrast to other emerging forms of "digital touch", such as artificial physical touch provided through haptic technologies. The visual touch regime is situated in complex professional and organisational practices involving particular ways of knowing that rely on the employment of 3D camera systems and 4D/"5D" scientific modelling. The authors address the knowledge and expertise issues pertaining to these new health technologies from a novel angle.

The chapter focuses not only on the enhancement of new capabilities, expertise, and functional work roles but on how new imaging technology may play a significant role in surgeons' and scientists' discovery of unexpected knowledge. Most of the interviewed surgeons not only work as medical doctors in the teaching hospitals but are also employed as scientists in associated medical departments, and their creative and artistic processes at work are fuelled by multidimensional imaging technologies. The authors argue that the discovery of unexpected knowledge is made possible because new highly detailed images are rendering the invisible visible and the imperceptible perceptible. In other words, the "visual touch" regime is directly coupled to the application of pre-existing knowledge as well as to the professional processes of creating new insight in medical discovery work and knowledge production. However, as I mentioned in the preface of this book, *serendipity* can be an ordinary experience—a pleasant surprise—for health professionals. It may also be an astonishing *WoW "Aha"* sensory-based experience, which better captures the innovative nature of knowledge production. As the authors demonstrate, this concept is tightly coupled to processes of organisational innovation. For example, the empirical study reveals that when professionals are applying visual touch by using the 4D OsiriX® system, they are able to render the unobservable observable in that they now see the heart's movements and are thus able to learn new facts concerning previously unknown variations in a patient's anatomy. In the elaborate analysis of the rich empirical data, the authors found that new multidimensional imaging technologies generate novel ways to perceive the world. In so doing, these systems create a foundation on which to develop new forms of knowledge work, that is, new expertise and professional understanding.

The authors conclude by pointing out that consideration should also be given to multisensory representations in future work. Emerging multisensory 4D and "5D" systems involve new applications that incorporate and reinstate human senses such as smell, touch, and taste with vision and hearing. The authors note that this domain is currently under-researched. At present, however, of all the human senses, vision ranks highest, as it is the most powerful source in gathering information about the surrounding world. The authors' focus on the dominance of the visual in medicine and science are therefore timely.

In Chap. 3, *Kimberly Jamie* examines the significant relocation of pharmacy work and the redistribution of professionals away from the traditional dispensary location to an increased presence in clinical locations. By drawing upon recent ethnographic work and interviews with community and hospital pharmacists in the UK, the study demonstrates how new ways of evaluative clinical work are accomplished. British pharmacies have undergone changes and re-configurations wherein a set of different health care technologies, such as dispensary robots and computerised prescribing and labelling devices, are reshaping day-to-day modern professional work.

In a key conception of *"technologies enabling clinical practice"*, the author demonstrates how new technologies enable the relocation of work in a more distributed fashion, such that professionals become less spatially bound to their traditional dispensary tasks. This relocation of work implies that professionals have more time to apply their expertise and increase their presence in the physical location of the consultation room (in the case of community pharmacies). In the case of hospital pharmacies, such relocation entails increased in-patient ward time at the bedside. The author argues that the implementation and realisation of relocated, technology-mediated pharmacy practices have been largely unexplored and thus deserve further analysis and conceptualisation.

The author's interview data nicely illustrate how a new form of technological monitoring, for example using blood glucose and carbon monoxide monitors, grants access to essential biomedical knowledge about patients' bodies. The interview data also describe how various technological devices provide patients with knowledge about their own bodies. While these new monitoring methods reduce the financial burden of drug-related readmissions, new practices are also creating new knowledge and are thus situated in an institutional context.

By adopting a contemporary science and technology studies approach, the author incorporates Normalisation Process Theory (NPT) into her analysis to explore the ways in which notions of '*reflexive monitoring*' and '*contextual integration*' can help provide conceptual anchors for understanding why some new technologies are normalised into everyday pharmacy practices and others are not. In so doing, this chapter not only demonstrates how new health care technologies make sense through changes in the management of medicines and financial pharmaceutical care strategies but also how these technologies reorganise professional relationships throughout the health care structure and transform everyday practices.

In Chap. 4, *Mohammadreza Rahimpour, Nigel H. Lovell, Branko G. Celler* and *John McCormick* discuss how a home tele-care management system can serve elderly homebound patients and how such new health care technologies redefine older peoples' social roles, some living alone and some living in rural villages and remote communities in metropolitan areas. In several succinct tables, the authors show how they have structured and analysed their data using concepts from a technology acceptance model. In particular, the authors identify and address stakeholder interests pertaining to patients' needs.

They provide a comprehensive view of in-home medical care and new medical equipment that has been developed to support older people and their caregivers. Their study also reflects great user diversity and accounts for the cultural diversity among elderly patients in the greater Sydney region. All patients included in the study had chronic diseases, such as congestive heart failure and chronic obstructive pulmonary disease. While older people often have less experience in interacting with technology, the authors demonstrate that this particular patient group may become more aware and knowledgeable of their health conditions by utilising emergent home tele-care systems that record key clinical indicators. In other words, by improving patients' knowledge about the states of their general health, they can also gain new insights into their diseases. Self-care, i.e., a patient's own health management, can thereby empower elderly patients and increase their participation in their health management. The information gained can serve as early warnings; it can notify patients of their health deterioration and also alert doctors to initiate emergency care services at an early stage.

These systems are designed and engineered to collect the patient's data, and the system thereafter presents and disseminates information about the patient's health status. In such a homecare service, patients become more involved in their own treatments, as they do some of the work at home that health care professionals previously carried out in clinics. As the authors discuss, this relocation of in-hospital treatments to distributed and remote homecare solutions saves costs and time by reducing the number of practitioner visits and results in less travelling for people living in remote areas, which in turn can result in a more effective usage of available resources in public health systems. However, implementing such emerging health care technologies in everyday settings is far from being a straightforward matter, not least because some elderly patients are unfamiliar with modern technological devices. According to the authors, this type of self-care services might have psychological costs in terms of anxiety due to elderly people having generally less experience in interacting with home-care technologies.

The authors found that anxiety, resistance to change, and technophobia are factors to consider in understanding technology acceptance and user assimilation. These factors can also explain user-resistance concerns associated with the use of home-care systems because of the patient's lack of understanding of how confidentiality is assured when personal data are transmitted to remote health professionals. As we move forward, the authors argue, it will also be imperative to investigate physicians' acceptance of self-care devices.

The authors of Chap. 5 discuss predictive, preventive and personalised medicine (PPPM) and how it may result in a re-configuration of our health care systems. *Morten Sager, Fredrik Bragesjö* and *Aant Elzinga* contrast some of the key notions of evidence-based medicine with person-centred medicine. Drawing on recent notions of health care governance, they discuss the fundamental health administration and policy project of speeding patient throughput through the health care system by individualising the prescribed medications and medical treatments to a patient's needs. The authors discuss the implications of rapid medical tests and diagnoses, which are beginning to revolutionise the diagnostic sector, and pharmacogenetically based knowledge in emerging diagnostic devices, which translate a patient's genetic profile into tailored treatments. Furthermore, rapid diagnoses promise major cost reductions, which are welcomed by health administrators. Such individual treatments could either be carried out by health care professionals at the point of care in hospitals and clinics or by the patients themselves outside of the hospital setting (e.g., in their home environment). The latter distributed form of technology-based treatment serves as a mediator in doctor-patient interactions and reduces hospital admissions. Distributed health care management of self-care treatments increase the flexibility in the provision of health care services as new technological devices allow patients to self-monitor their vital indicators and prescribed health parameters (see, e.g., self-use toolkits for diseases such as Type 2 diabetes, hypertonia, and secondary hyperlipidaemia or hypercholesterolemia).

In particular, the authors discuss the recent technological developments in relation to how the distribution of expertise is re-configured and re-negotiated within new expert-patient interfaces and relationships. In light of the current technological and health care institutional developments, the authors contrast the traditional role of medical knowledge and expertise in relation to new, technologically mediated and distributed forms of physician-patient interplay in self-care and telemedicine activities.

The chapter presents a conceptual framework that falls within the realm of science and technology studies. It includes three key theoretical and analytical lenses. These three lenses provide conceptual anchors to address the greater issue of emerging applications in self-care and telemedicine. The authors' re-conceptualisation of expertise is a fruitful way to define the future scope of PPPM and to better understand how profoundly technology changes the production of new knowledge and the self-understanding of patients.

The authors apply their framework to the reconsideration of an empirical case study of self-care devices that are being used to overcome physical distances.

Distributed care, if organised properly, has the potential to simultaneously orchestrate numerous medical expertise domains in different geographical locations. Like *Rahimpour* et al. (Chap. 4), the authors are concerned with how technology facilitates the exchange of information and patient data between different levels of expertise (ranging from specialists to general practitioners), thus finding ways to reduce response times to critical events and delivering better system efficiency. By providing up-to-date information on a patient's status, the doctor can monitor patients on a regular basis and prevent or reduce the number of emergency visits and hospital admissions.

The authors demonstrate the tension between evidence-based knowledge that is promoted by medical specialists on the one hand and the personal knowledge of patients on the other. In summary, the chapter describes how experts and patients enter new distributed relationships in a number of emerging health technologies that are changing traditional "expert repertoires". With self-managing patients (i.e., self-regulated care), the division between expert and lay knowledge changes. The authors note how the traditional role of the doctor shifts from the delivery of care services to supervising the care. More broadly, this case touches on the issue of preventive medicine, wherein technological systems support independent living, as well as how this development can increase access to health care and how medicine can play a more predictive and preventive role in the future.

References

Adner, R., & Levinthal, D. A. (2002). The emergence of emerging technologies. *California Management Review, 45*(1), 50–66.

Baaij, M., Van Den Bosch, F., & Volberda, H. (2004). The international relocation of corporate centres: Are corporate centres sticky? *European Management Journal, 22*(2), 141–149.

Berger, P. L., & Luckmann, T. (1967). *The social construction of reality.* London: Anchor Books.

Boje, D. M. (2006). What happened on the way to postmodern? *Qualitative Research in Organization and Management: An International Journal, 1*(1), 22–40.

Burnes, B. (2004). *Managing change* (4th ed.). Harlow: Financial Times Prentice Hall.

Collins English Dictionary (2010) *30th Anniversary Edition*, (10th ed.) London.

Daniels, J.(2011). *Assured Identity for the Cloud.* Doctoral Thesis. College of Technology. Indiana State University.

Deleuze, G., & Guattari, F. (2004). *A thousands plateaus.* London: Continuum.

Edwards, P. (2010). *A vast machine: Computer models, climate data, and the politics of global warming.* Cambridge: MIT Press.

Ericsson, A. K., Prietula, M. J., & Cokely, E. T.(July–August, 2007). The making of an expert. *Harvard Business Review 85*(7/8), 114–121.

Foucault, M. (1973). *The birth of the clinic: An archaeology of medical perception.* London: Routledge.

Fridlund, M.(1999). *Den gemensamma utvecklingen. Staten, storföretagen och samarbetet kring den svenska elkrafttekniken.* Avhandling. Stockholm: Brutus Östlings Bokförlag.

Greener, T., & Hughes, M. (2006). Managing change before change management. *Strategic Change, 15*(4), 205–212.

Groll, R., Baker, R., & F. Moss (2002). Quality improvement research: Understanding the science of change in health care. *BMJ Quality and Safety in Health Care, 11*(2), 110–111.

Hatch, M. J. (1997). *Organization theory: Modern, symbolic, and postmodern perspectives.* Oxford: Oxford University Press.

Hatch, M. J. (2011). *Organisations: A Very Short Introduction.* Oxford: Oxford University Press.

Heimer Rathbone, C. L. (2012). *Ready for change? Transition through turbulence to reformation and transformation.* Basingstoke: Palgrave Macmillan.

Lave, J., & Wenger, E. (1991). *Situated learning: Legitimate peripheral participation.* Cambridge: Cambridge University Press.

Leavitt, H. J. (1965). Applying organizational change in industry: Structural, technological, and humanistic approaches. In G. M. James (Ed.), *Handbook of organizations.* Chicago: Rand McNally.

Linstead, S., & Thanem, T. (2007). Multiplicity, virtuality and organization: The contribution of gilles deleuze. *Organization Studies, 28*(10), 1483–1501.

Livesey, G. (2005). Assemblage. In A. Parr (Ed.), *The deleuze dictionary* (pp. 18–19). New York: Columbia University Press.

Marshak, R. J. (2005). Contemporary challenges to the philosophy and practice of organizational development. In L. D. Bradford & W. W. Burke (Eds.), *Reinventing organizational development: New approaches to change in organizations.* San Francisco: Pfeiffer.

McNulty, T., & Ferlie, E. (2002). *Reengineering health care: The complexities of organizational transformation.* Oxford: Oxford University Press.

Mondada, L. (2003). Working with video: How surgeons produce video records of their actions. *Visual Studies, 18*(1), 58–73.

OECD Health Project. (2005). *Health technologies and decision making.* Paris: Organisation for Economic Co-operation and Development.

Office of Technology Assessment (1976). *Development of medical technology: Opportunities for assessment.* August 1976. Washington DC.

Oxford Dictionaries (2011). *Concise Oxford English Dictionary,* (12th ed.) Oxford.

Pearson, S., & Charlesworth, A. (2009). Accountability as a way forward for privacy protection in the cloud. In M. G. Jaatun, G. Zhao, & C. Rong (Eds.), *Cloud computing* (pp. 131–144). Berlin: Springer.

Roback, K. (2006). *Medical device innovation: The integrated process of invention, diffusions, and deployment.* Linköping: Linköping University.

Rystedt, H., Ivarsson, J., Asplund, S., Allansdotter Johansson, A., & Båth, M. (2011). Rediscovering radiology: New technologies and remedial action at the worksite. *Social Studies of Science, 41*(6), 867–891.

Schillmeier, M., & Domènech, M. (Eds.). (2010). *New technologies and emerging spaces of care.* Aldershot: Ashgate.

Simon, H. A. (1987). The steam engine and the computer: What makes technology revolutionary. *EDUCOM Bulletin, 22*(1), 2–5.

Sørensen, B. M. (2005). Immaculate defecation: Gilles Deleuze and Félix Guattari in organization theory. *The Sociological Review, 53,* 120–133.

Styhre, A. (2005). Deleuze, desire and motivation theory. In J. Brewis, S. Linstead, A. O'Shea, & D. M. Boje (Eds.), *The passion of organizing.* Oslo: Abstrakt.

Styhre, A. (2010a). Organizing technologies of vision: Making the invisible visible in media-laden observations. *Information and Organization, 20,* 64–78.

Styhre, A. (2010b). *Visual culture in organizations.* New York: Taylor & Francis.

Targama, A., & Wasen, K. (2005). Mutual intelligibility and sensemaking: Theorizing in action. In K. Wasen (Ed.), *Knowledge production in mergers and takeover.* Gothenburg: BAS Publishing House.

Tracey, W. R. (2003). *The human resource glossary: The complete desk reference for hr executives, managers, and practitioners* (3rd ed.). London: St. Lucie Press.

Tsoukas, H., & Chia, R. (2002). On organizational becoming: Rethinking organizational change. *Organization Science, 13*(5), 567–582.

Van de Ven, A. H. (1991). *The process of adopting innovations in organizations: Three cases of hospital innovations, in: people and technology in the workplace.* Washington: National Academy Press.

Wasen, K. (2005). Person-friendly robot interaction: Social, psychological and technological issues in health care work. In *Proceedings of 14th IEEE RO-MAN* (pp. 643–648). August 13–15, Nashville.

Wasen, K. (2010). Replacement of highly educated surgical assistants by robot technology in working life: Paradigm shift in the service sector. *International Journal of Social Robotics, 2*(4), 431–438. doi:10.1007/s12369-010-0062-y.

Wasen, K. (Ed.). (2012). *Knowledge production in mergers and acquisitions* (2nd ed.). Gothenburg: BAS Publishing House.

Webster, A. (2007). *Health, technology and society: A sociological critique*. Gordonsville: Palgrave Macmillan.

Chapter 2
The Visual Touch Regime: Real-Time 3D Image-Guided Robotic Surgery and 4D and "5D" Scientific Illustration at Work

Kristian Wasen and Meaghan Brierley

Abstract Emerging multidimensional imaging technologies (3D/4D/"5D") open new ground for exploring visual worlds and rendering new image-based knowledge, especially in areas related to medicine and science. 3D imaging is defined as three visual dimensions. 4D imaging is three visual dimensions plus time. 4D imaging can also be combined with functional transitions (i.e., following radioactive tracer isotope through the body in positron emission tomography). 4D imaging plus functionality is defined as "5D" imaging. We propose the idea of "visual touch", a conceptual middle ground between touch and vision, as a basis for future explorations of contemporary institutional standards of image-based work. "Visual touch" is both the process of reconciling the senses (human and artificial) and the end result of this union of the senses. We conclude that while new multi-dimensional imaging technology emphasises vision, new forms of image-based work using visual materials cannot solely be classified as "visual".

Keywords Display technology • Visual perception • In situ image guidance • Senses • Innovative knowledge • Scientific illustration • Image-guided robotic surgery

2.1 Bringing Vision and Visuality into Business and Management Studies

New work practices in the use of vision are emerging as the dominant workplace regimes in the institutional landscape. But business scholars still lack a theoretical language to describe and understand the present dynamics of modern

K. Wasen (✉)
University of Gothenburg, Gothenburg, Sweden
e-mail: kristian.wasen@gu.se

M. Brierley
University of Calgary, Calgary, AB, Canada

K. Wasen (ed.), *Emerging Health Technology*, SpringerBriefs in Health Care Management and Economics, DOI: 10.1007/978-3-642-32570-0_2, © The Author(s) 2013

practices of vision and of current production standards for image-guided goods and services.

> Vision and visuality are emerging in many forms and ... [have] a central role in the functioning of organizations. Since human vision is to some extent always already present, it is somewhat paradoxically also what is somewhat taken for granted and overlooked (no pun intended); it is an "absent present" in organization theory. Always all-too-mundane to be noticed, yet largely theoretically unexplored, vision is what deserves a proper analysis and a proper theory. (Styhre 2010b, p. 19)

We live in an increasingly image-based professional world but vision has not been fully scrutinised in empirical field studies or explicitly developed in theoretical management studies. Imaging and visualization is an increasingly important area of investigation in science and technology studies (STS): images are shown to help professionals define theories (Nersessian 2008); relocate and share ideas (Galison 1997; Henderson 1999; Knorr Cetina 2001; Latour 1990); and communicate with disparate audiences (Burri and Dumit 2008; Landau et al. 2009). Images have become increasingly important in medicine (Engström and Selenger 2009), where diagnostic imagery is invaluable to diagnosing patients (Joyce 2005; Mol 2002) and conducting treatment.

The social studies of imaging technology and visualization raise important questions about how images come to be, and how images intersect with different forms of knowledge about ourselves and our world (Burri and Dumit 2008; Daston and Galison 2007). Human knowledge is deeply entrenched in "traditions of seeing", which is reflected in various notions ranging from "professional vision" (Goodwin 1994), "visual knowledge" (Cohn 2007), and imaged knowledge (Beaulieu 2003).

In the field of management and business studies, Alexander Styhre, a scholar in organisation theory, explores regimes of visuality and provides theories about the requirement for skilled vision in certain practices by situating these practices in historical, cultural, and organisational settings (Styhre 2010a, b). For Styhre, vision is far from being a straightforward matter or a trivial phenomenon in organisational life. Styhre argues it is important to outline specific forms of vision(s) in the workplace, a view with which we concur. Our research attempts to fill some of the gaps in the understanding of vision and visuality and thereby shed new light on the concepts. Our conceptual analysis is empirically anchored on what anthropologist Geertz (1983) calls the "thick descriptions" of real-life practices of seeing. Our case demonstrates that in situ "multi-dimensional visual touch" is an emerging and distinctive form of visuality in the technology-mediated work environments of robotic surgery and scientific imaging.

Robotic technologies and advanced imaging technologies have redefined surgical work, resulting in a dilemma in current surgical practice as to how the use of human senses is being redefined. The purpose of this chapter is to introduce, explain, and empirically explore the reorganisation of interactions in medical practice in the use of visually guided robotic surgery. The process of introducing new technologies changes the priority of the senses and the knowledge that is lost and gained. The integration of various forms of advanced robotic and imaging technologies into surgical practice involves a profound shift in focus for surgeons away from traditional manual surgery. (Wasen 2010) The transition involves a change from the use of physical sensation (i.e., tactile feedback) in traditional surgery to a dependence on visual feedback in robotic surgery. Although it promises increased precision, stability, and control, computer-integrated robotic surgery can be challenging because surgeons can no longer depend on their sense of touch. This change-induced dilemma represents a point of 'organisational transformation'—the need to adjust standard human or professional practices in new and unexpected ways.

Our interest in robotic technology and 3D and 4D imaging[1] is based on how these influence surgical practice and professional visual expertise. We explore how the use of technology has been adjusted to fit certain surgical needs and how surgeons' preferences have been addressed and continue to be addressed. By allowing the surgeons' experiences and perspectives to guide our findings, we aim to contribute to discussions of visually guided robotic surgery and how it affects established professional embodied knowledge. Increasingly detailed and comprehensive images and videos are being produced, leading to enhanced visual attention and immersion. This transition is rendering the invisible visible and the unobservable observable. From our perspective, practices of observing and knowing in multi-sensorial worlds are coupled with the serendipitous findings in the medical and other scientific fields.

The chapter is structured into five sections. First, we justify the importance of examining the work performed by professionals. We draw on the scientific literature pertaining to organisational knowledge and innovation management. Second, we provide a brief historical overview of surgery and the introduction of robotic techniques and imaging to surgery. Third, we present prior research on individual established knowledge in professional work and on image-guided medicine. The fourth section introduces empirical cases of image-guided robotic surgery and the increasingly important shift in importance of the sense of touch in the transition from traditional to imaging practices. The description includes reactions from surgeons to this transition. In the discussion, we position multi-dimensional scientific imaging and image-guided robotic surgery as institutional standards for image-based work. We conclude that while new multi-dimensional imaging technology puts an emphasis on vision, new forms of image-based work with visual materials cannot solely be classified as "visual".

We challenge the common perception regarding the distinction between vision and touch and propose that the line between the two is in fact blurred, given that touch in this context is defined as "touching with the eye" (i.e., a form of "tactile vision") rather than limited to only the physical touch. "Touching with the eye"

---

[1] 3D imaging is defined as three visual dimensions. 4D imaging is three visual dimensions plus time. 4D imaging can also be combined with functional transitions (i.e., following radioactive tracer isotope through the body in positron emission tomography). 4D imaging plus functionality is defined by the OsirixX® DICOM Viewer as "5D" imaging.

should not be equated with the more general notion of "digital touch", which is used for haptic technology (see, e.g., Paterson 2005). Therefore, the employment of advanced visual technology reconfigures and redefines the meaning and uses of vision and touch. We propose the concept of "visual touch", a conceptual middle ground between touch and vision, as a basis for future explorations of contemporary institutional regimes of image-based work. "Visual touch" is both the process of reconciling the senses (human and artificial) and the end result of this sensorial union. Finally, consideration is given to the generalisability of our analysis when determining how other multi-sensorial work practices should be studied.

2.2 Organisational Knowledge

The knowledge creation process reflects the dynamic and emergent nature of organisational innovation. As Davenport and Prusak succinctly put it, "ALL HEALTHY organizations generate and use knowledge. As organisations interact with their environments, they absorb information, turn it into knowledge, and take action based on it in combination with their experiences, values, and internal rules. They sense and respond. Without knowledge, an organisation could not organize itself; it would be unable to maintain itself as a functioning enterprise." (1998, s. 52) The organisational innovation view includes cultural heritage, social interaction, communication, and decision-making (Wejnert 2002; Rogers 2003; Kincaid 2004). Attention is also paid to the tangible and intangible dimensions of knowledge work as well as the work environment. This view is echoed by Tornatzky and Fleischer (1990, p.10) who maintain that the term "innovation" should be understood as "the situationally new development and introduction of knowledge-derived tools, artefacts, and devices by which people extend and interact with their environment".

Barley and Kunda question the lack of focus on people's day-to-day actions in management and organization studies. "The dearth of data on what people actually do—the skills, knowledge, and practices that comprise their routine work—leaves us with increasing anachronistic theories and outdated images of work and how it is organized." (2001, p. 90). Barley and Kunda argue that it is not sufficient to interview practitioners as to their practices and that scholars must also observe how work is accomplished in the workplace. In a wider sense, innovations constitute new work methods, social and cultural practices and even new ideas or new ways of thinking and perceiving the world. The generation of new knowledge in surgical practices proves useful when it is adopted, augmented, applied and passed on in an organisational setting. As Nonaka and Takeuchi observed, "When organizations innovate, they do not simply process information, from the outside in, in order to solve existing problems and adapt to a changing environment. They actually create new knowledge and information, from the inside out, in order to redefine both problems and solutions and, in the process, to re-create their environment." (1995, p. 56) Organisational innovation is unlike technological innovation in that it focuses on changes in routine human activities rather than on the process of invention (Freeman 1994).[2]

Organisational innovations, as symbols and perceptions, may be viewed as the human endeavour to incorporate new technologies into specific professional, organisational and cultural environments. Technological change follows when an innovation is put into practice and replaces old habits with new routines. The use of imaging in health care is not only the use of a novel technology but also the cessation of existing work practices in favour of newer, more effective ones. Organisational innovation can also act as a form of path dependency; the decisions made in the past influence and limit the options for action in the present.

2.3 Surgery, the Early Use of Robotics, and Reinstating Binocular Vision

The evolution of medicine in general, and the art of surgery in particular, traces its history back to the ancient Greeks. Indeed, the making of surgical equipment and instruments has a long historical tradition of skilled craftsmanship (e.g., Göranzon et al. 1987). These semi-specialised tools enhance the manipulative capacity of the surgeon's hands and represent extensions of the human body (cf. Mumford 1934, 1952). The era of modern surgical practice has commonly been referred to as either the period following the introduction of antiseptics/aseptics (Bynum and Porter 1993; Harding-Rains 1977) or the post-anaesthetics period (Cartwright 1967; Sullivan 1996). The subsequent post-modern era of surgical practice began with the adoption of complex remote manipulation technology (cf. Bicker et al. 2004), which included the use of robotics. For Bicker et al. (2004. p. 391) and colleagues, remote handling "has its roots in some of our most primitive tools… Blacksmiths tongs are a crude, but effective example of an early remote handling tool." Being able to extend one's reach into a hostile environment is a valuable ability when one still wants to control the position and orientation of materials

---

[2] Hawkins and Verhoest (2002) discuss a considerable body of research showing that techno-logical and organisational change are highly interconnected. The characteristics of innovation, as laid out in the OECD Analytical Report on Technology, Productivity and Job Creation (OECD 1996), clearly demonstrate that technological change "calls for and results from institutional and organisational change". Hawkins and Verhoest's approach is consistent with the one pre-sented by OECD (1994), but their approach more explicitly emphasises discovering how firms and organisations use technology in order to extend our knowledge. However, we do realize that there may be a limitation in the use of the term "organisational innovation" as it closely resem-bles the notion of the "social invention of the organisation" (Pedersen and Dobbin, 1997). Other related concepts, such as "social innovation" or "non-technological innovation", are more or less consistent with the term "social invention". These concepts are somewhat problematic as most advanced work settings assemble various technological devices and social practices, which tightly interweave the social, organisational, and technological.

while working (Vertut and Coiffet 1985). Telemanipulation extends the human operator's reach into remote environments while focusing on ease of manipulation and meeting the sense requirements for participating effectively. Manipulation involves manual dexterity, judgment and intelligence, which are governed by practice and the senses.

At the beginning of the 21st century, the innovative use of robotics enabled the exploration of remote places not previously accessible to humans. Space robots navigating the moon or at the bottom of the sea are well-known examples, but recently, robots have begun exploring new frontiers inside the human body. To be able to navigate in such remote areas, robots must be interlinked with sophisticated visualisation technologies.

Since the beginning of traditional invasive surgery, and even before the evolution of specially designed operating theatres, human touch has been a key feature in treating patients. Robotic technology has only recently entered the operating theatre, releasing surgeons from old constraints such as limited human vision and the lack of precise hand movements. At the same time, however, the technology has created new constraints, such as precluding the use of tactile information and stereoscopic vision during surgery. This highlights an increasingly important area in the study of imaging and visualisation as to how to replicate binocular vision and touch. The history medical and surgical imaging spans centuries of anatomical depiction (Oldfield and Landon 2006; Roberts and Tomlinson 1992; Tsafrir and Ohry 2001), artist/surgeon collaborations (Crosby and Cody 1991) and more recent bodily explorations with computed tomography (CT), magnetic resonance imaging (MRI), and positron emission tomography (PET) (Holtzmann-Kevles 1997; Marchessault and Sawchuk 2000). Imaging technologies transform the body into data, revealing what cannot be observed by unaided human senses, and providing information for an expanded understanding of imaging results. These technologies present an opportunity to discover new relationships that are "productive of new relations" (Beaulieu 2003). The current challenge with modern surgical technology is how to use imaging to improve upon the surgeon's finely honed abilities.

2.3.1 Depth and Presence Through Stereoscopic Imaging

The ability to perceive depth is the innate ability of binocular vision. The slightly different images captured by the eyes are reconciled by the brain to provide an illusion of depth (Fig. 2.1). Stereoscopic imaging in surgery is fundamentally different from the common understanding of 3D imaging, which is often only the 2D representation of a 3D object. Surgery and medicine have strived to attain quality stereoscopic representations since the late 1800s (Getty and Green 2007) and have successfully used stereopsis in training and in practice (Davidson 1916; Brodke and Randolph 2003; Held and Hui 2011; Hofmeister et al. 2001; Lee et al. 2010; Marescaux and Soler 2004; Oleynikov et al. 2005; Patel et al. 2008; Xing et al.

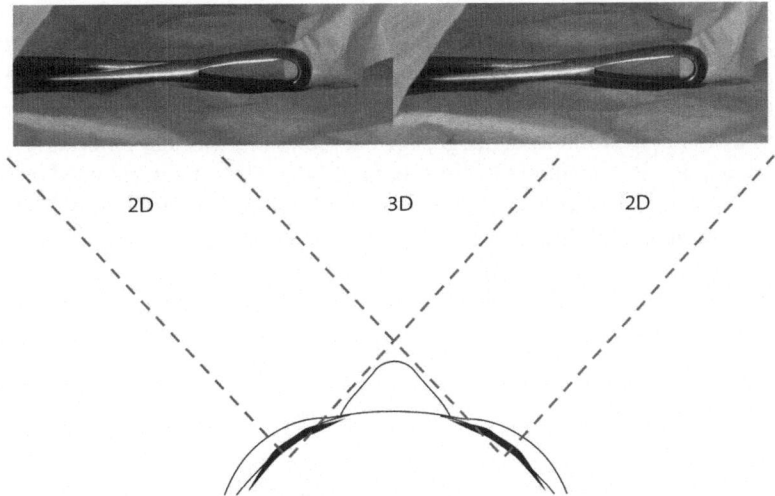

Fig. 2.1 Stereoscopic images are a result of binocular vision where eyes that are placed a distance apart are used together. Each eye sees a different image (2D), and the brain reconciles these images to produce a sense of depth and three dimensions (3D). © M. Brierley

2009; Morton 1989). These authors have attempted to achieve "enhanced shape perception in the absence of other visual cues, whether the application is diagnostics, trainings, or remote surgery" (Held and Hui 2011).

The need for stereoscopic imaging lies not only in improved imaging but also in improved navigation of a physical space by replicating the spatial understanding previously gained through touch.

The ability to precisely navigate 3D space is lost when binocular vision is not available and when the space under consideration cannot be touched. Stereoscopic approaches to surgery provide alternatives for both the loss of binocular vision and the loss of touch.

Images used to plan, guide, and review surgery take on an integral role in these procedures. Companies that create stereoscopic imaging technologies offer new sites for development of computer-mediated life sciences (Myers 2008) and changes in their practices. Professional practices change as stereoscopic imaging in robotic surgery become closely integrated with work of surgeons.

2.3.2 The Role of Visual Embodied Knowledge in Professional Work

Visual knowledge may depend on the specific competences required by specific technologies (Cohn 2007), or it can have an intangible quality, such as a pervasive personal element that cannot be observed or touched, that is embodied in people, artefacts and actions (Bal 2003). Blackler (1995) argues that knowledge is linked to actions, indicating that its value lies in its use. Polanyi (1967/2009) introduced the term "tacit knowledge" to describe an experiential knowledge that cannot be written down. It is (1) embodied knowledge, such as the ability to hold a pencil or (2) contextual knowledge, for example, the way the laboratory setting gives knowledge its meaning (Knorr Cetina 2001). Thus, tacit knowledge is both somatic (a physical routine) and collective (a cultural practice) (Collins 2010).

The intangible skill of surgical practice is described as a skill developed through experience and maturity, a skill that some people call "intuition" (Cohn 2007, p. 93). Surgeons feel as much as see their way through surgical procedures.

2.3.3 The Senses

Part of the change dilemma in surgical practice today is how the senses are being redefined. In robotic surgery, touch is mediated through images and machines at a distance from the patient. Research has linked the senses to culture (Howes 2005; Classen 1993; Feld 2005), to memory (Bergson 1908/1988), and to the situated environment (Feld 2005). McLuhan pointed out that "[a]ny culture is an order of sensory preferences."[3] Others have examined lived experiences as involving shifts in sensory, multi-sensory or cross-sensory experiences (Feld 2005, pp. 180; Newell and Shams 2007; Shams et al. 2000) and considered how our experience over a lifetime decides our cultural understanding of the senses (Howes 2005). We know physical space through how our body exists in that space (Bourdieu 1977), which is also part of memory. Steven Feld highlights the work of Bergson (1908/1988) when he writes that memory is the "thousand details out of our past experience" (Feld 2005, p. 81).

Out of these explorations arises an important question about the senses and how they are attuned to taken-for-granted activities in professional worlds and between people. By recognizing changes in sense emphasis in a changing surgical environment (touch as mediated by image and robot, rather than direct surgeon-patient interaction), we can scrutinize the theoretical positions that guide our conceptions of senses and knowledge. As Rosenberger (2011) recently maintained, "Technologies provide mediation between our bodies and the world, changing our perceptual abilities ...how humans embody technology, and how technological embodiment transforms human experience" (Rosenberger 2011, p. 13). Furthermore, Myers (2008) reminds us of Merleau-Ponty's (1962) phenomenology of perception where "sensation and movement are intimately tied to visual understandings of form" (Myers 2008, p. 166). The empirical part of this study pays particular attention to the practices of seeing and touching mediated through multi-dimensional imaging in the surgical domain. In the empirical context, where surgeons' movements change with new technologies, so must their perceptual approaches and their embodied understandings of surgery itself.

---

[3] The Playboy Interview: Marshall McLuhan", Playboy Magazine, March 1969.

This chapter attempts to fill some of these gaps in our understanding by examining how change is understood from the point of view of practitioners; how an emerging technology influences user perspectives, knowledge, and practices; and how those in an established medical profession interpret and negotiate these changes.

Ethnography that focuses on the senses in particular accounts for how multi-sensoriality is "integral" to people's daily work and lives (Pink 2009, pp. 1–2). This method examines how the senses work in gaining and navigating knowledge. Methodologically, our chapter contributes to these efforts by promoting the benefits of cross-disciplinary research in the realm of workplace studies.

2.4 The Case: From 2D Imaging to 3D Stereoscopic Cameras and 4D/5D Surgical Imaging In Vivo

The late 20th and early 21st centuries have seen a rapid proliferation of powerful robotic systems in healthcare, systems designed to exceed the surgeon's limitations. While the human eye is an astonishing "depth-seeing apparatus" (Jastrow 1936), its field of vision is limited due to optical glare and other factors. The power of robotic systems also lies in their ability to become extensions of the human body and thereby allow operators to work remotely, thus enabling human expertise to be applied in physical spaces that were previously unreachable. Bicker noted, ".... although relatively complex mechanisms, when well maintained and used by skilled operatives, these devices can be used to undertake highly dexterous and extremely precise tasks" (Bicker et al. 2004, p. 394).

In the case of robotic surgery, for example, robotic arms can hold sophisticated camera systems steady. Even when the surgeon is working directly on a patient's body through a robot, the risk of danger to internal organs is still present, and therefore, a "gentle human touch" during surgery is still necessary. If a surgeon is performing open surgery on a patient in a standard operating theatre, all members of the team can view the operation and see how it is proceeding. In traditional surgery, if an event occurs in the surgeon's periphery, the event is still within the surgeon's direct vision (see Fig. 2.2). These circumstances are representative of surgical procedures before two-dimensional (2D) imaging.

The transition from manual open surgery to manual laparoscopic surgery (i.e., keyhole surgery) marked a profound change to 2D imaging. This new imaging technique relied on a change in hand-eye coordination that often took surgeons years to acquire proficiency and expertise in handling to efficiently master the use of manual laparoscopic instruments. Moreover, working with 2D images in keyhole surgery was a challenge because most television screens did not have good contrast resolution. As Fig. 2.3 illustrates, the lead surgeon would often encounter visual noise on the mounted television screens and would lack a sense of depth when using laparoscopic surgery.

Non-invasive approaches, to which robot technology belongs, have dramatically altered the traditional methods surgeons have used to sterilise and use

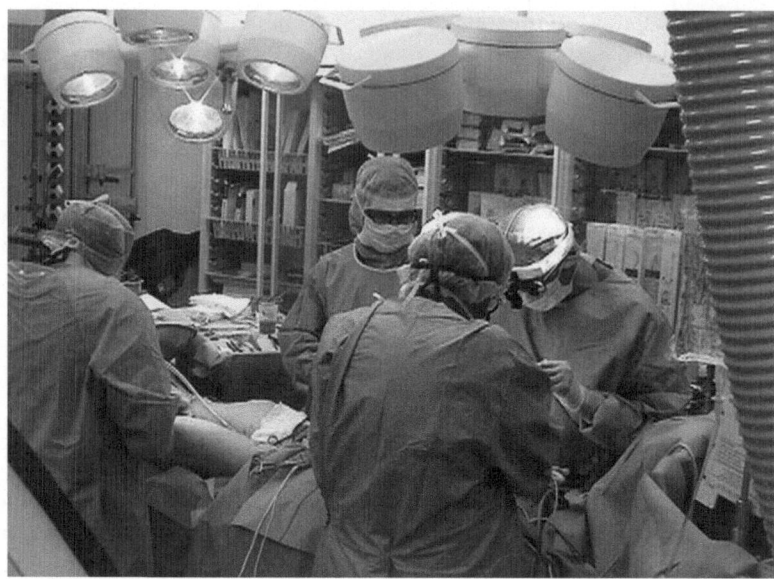

Fig. 2.2 Traditional open-heart surgery requires that surgeons and assistants work on a patient in close proximity with one another. In a standard mitral valve operation, assistants interact directly with the head surgeon (far right). © K. Wasen

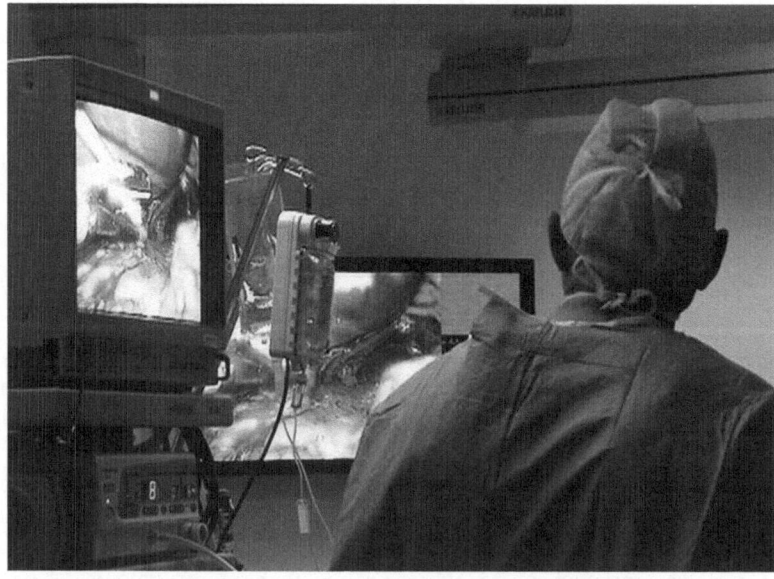

Fig. 2.3 Two non-stereoscopic 2-D images of the cameras in laparoscopic surgery. © K Wasen

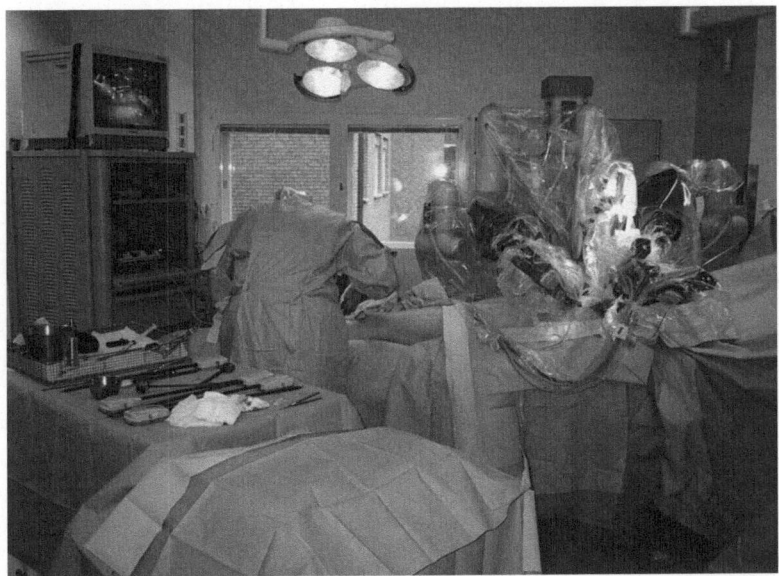

Fig. 2.4 The robotic arms occupy the space around the patient where the head surgeon and surgical assistants would normally stand (see Fig. 2.2). In robotic mitral valve surgery, the head surgeon controls the robot remotely through a console. Although assisting staff members are more spread out in the operating theatre, they are still required to be in close proximity to the patient and the robotic arms. © K. Wasen

their instruments and the methods employed for operating on their patients. (see Figs. 2.4 and 2.5) A surgeon explained this new approach as follows: "As we become less invasive, we are not putting our hands inside the patients as much at all." Thus, physical contact with the patient is lost with the new system. An obvious advantage motivating non-invasive approaches is the improved aseptic or sterile environment they provide. While the promises of technological mediation in robot surgery are increased precision, stability, and control, the transition from traditional open surgery to robotic surgery is challenging because surgeons can no longer use their tactile sensation. A urologist expressed a similar concern:

> You cannot feel. It is easier to feel things; it is easier to operate if you can feel things. You can feel how thick the tissue is, you can dissect with your hands. When you are tying something or dissecting something, you can feel how much tension you are applying to the tissues. You get none of that with the robot; you do not get any tactile feedback from the robot. It almost feels the same; no matter how hard you are pushing, it feels the same on the robot.

For all of the interviewees, the direct loss of physical contact during an operation with the patient's bodies in general, and patient's internal organs in particular, has had several direct negative consequences. A thoracic surgeon found that non-invasive approaches in robotic surgery have made his work much harder in that "It is a big difference that you cannot feel, there is no tactile feedback."

Fig. 2.5 The head surgeon works at the robotic console remotely from the patient and the surgical team. The *left* image presents the upper console interface where the surgeon views the 3-dimensional imagery and interacts with the hand controls. The *right* image presents the foot controls. The console is able to operate remotely and can be placed outside the operating theatre or even outside the hospital. © K. Wasen

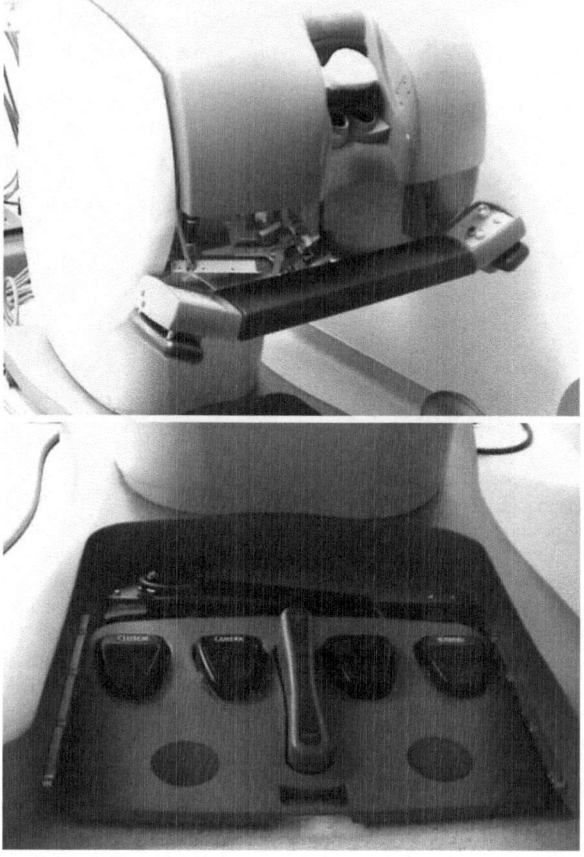

This study demonstrates how surgical robot technology fundamentally alters the way physicians use their different senses when operating on and interacting with patients through technological mediation during surgical procedures. More specifically, robot surgery entails a profound shift in focus for surgeons in their traditional manual procedures, from a reliance on physical sensation (i.e., tactile feedback) in traditional open surgery to increased dependence on visual feedback.

2.4.1 Compensation with Superior Artificial Visualisation

Professional competences in the surgical domain integrate with the new and unfamiliar high-tech demands of robotic applications, and this may mean replacing an advanced understanding of touch with a developed comprehension of visual data.

First, surgeons must learn and adapt to a new task routine in the operating theatre. Second, the transition from manual hands-on surgery to remote robotics is not easy and requires a different type of hand-eye coordination skill. Third, the case of robotic surgery points to the fact that not everyone can benefit from this new technology. A large part of the success of the operation relies on professional knowledge to analyse and understand the detailed 3-dimensional images as well as the surgeon's ability to use the sophisticated 3-dimensional camera system in an optimal manner. For this reason, it is paramount that new surgical trainees are taught how to use robotic systems and learn the proper role of these systems in the contemporary operating theatre.

The transition from human to robotic touch and from human to 3D magnified vision alters the use and purpose of the senses in surgical practices. Robotic technology in a medical setting supports and extends a surgeon's visual capabilities, promotes a dependence on visual media, and requires surgeons to work more independently (human to robot rather than human to human). Just as humans have created an ability to touch and manipulate what could not previously be observed through robotic support, so has robotic technology changed our practices and our needs.

> I think adjusting to using visual cues about the tension on tissues and things like that are very important. But, on the other hand, about technology, is that people insist "well, you know, my tactile sensation is better than your visual". I do not think that has been proven. I would argue that there are probably more benefits to magnification in many sorts of cases than there are to tactile feeling.

The above surgeon explicitly questioned the traditional reliance upon physical feedback as an important prerequisite to do a satisfactory job. For unskilled hands and for most inexperienced residents working in surgical clinics, such tactile sensations would be exceeding difficult to fully perceive. In contrast, experienced and knowledgeable physicians could easily discern the same anatomical details by touching them. The surgeon quoted above also maintained that enhanced human vision is far superior to any tactile ability.

> I think that in many surgeons' hands, they overestimate the importance of their tactile feeling simply because they have never done without it. As technology advances, there will be new ways to look at things, such as looking at if you can use a probe to determine if an area is malignant or not. Is that not better than your fingers? So, why not?

Surgeons have noted that in conventional open procedures, they were able, at least to some extent, to have extraordinary magnification of the surgical area. As observed during video-documented conventional open procedures, surgeons commonly had loupes positioned on top of their heads (i.e., a pair of specially designed magnifying glasses attached in front of their eyes; see Fig. 2.2). When using these types of "sensory enhancing equipment" (McLuhan 1964), a surgeon's centre of attention still remained on a small part of the entire wound, an area that would be invisible to the naked eye. Hence, visual perception is gained either by using a pair of magnifying glasses or optical camera systems. As one urological surgeon noted, such visual magnification also renders some things imperceptible because, as he explained, "… you are looking at a tunnel vision event where you see only a direct vision of what the camera is looking at. You do not see left and right, you see only a direct tunnel vision." This surgeon suggests that there is an increased reliance on selective non-direct visual images from the two cameras inside the patient. The visual selectiveness is experienced as positive because it actually enables the surgeon to focus on what is happening inside the patient's body. As the urological surgeon notes, "You are extraordinarily focused on this one spot [of the entirety of the wound] with the robot. There is no question about that. But I think that the amplification of it is so much greater because of the [three-dimensional] magnification, so you have to be cognizant of where everything is around you because you are only seeing a small area."

Surgeons who have had extensive experience operating under the old regime of manual procedure noticed initially that increased immersion also resulted in a narrower field of vision. In practice, a 3-dimensional view of the surgical field in robot surgery provides surgeons with the possibility of an even greater sense of screening their sensory awareness from other external inputs.

New imaging technology supports the surgeons' need for extraordinary focus in their job. In other words, the material configurations of the imaging technology render certain aspects perceptible and allow physicians to notice details that they had previously just assumed would be there. For example, various small nerves and blood vessels in the human body are almost invisible to the naked eye.

With robotic surgery, however, enhanced artificial magnification provides greater visual amplification than was provided by loupes in traditional open surgery. As one assistant thoracic surgeon described in reference to the vast difference between open and robotic surgery in terms of improved 3D visualisation, "The magnification, and your ability to discern structures, is almost microscopic in nature". Another surgeon described it this way:

> So, in principle at least, the robot gives you a big advantage there because it actually gives you the opportunity to focus on exactly what you are doing and still get information in digital format or in audio format, visually on the screen or just from a microphone of what is going on around the room … Of course, it is a different type of feeling, which may be a little bit scary for the surgeon in the beginning because he does not, for example, see the whole heart.

Despite the experience being "scary" at first, the above quoted surgeon repeatedly refers to the advantages of an increased ability to focus. This suggests that 3D imaging in surgical work demands focus, but this may be related to the technology employed. Bicker et al. (2004) observes that the use of tele-operated technology brings a dramatic increase in mental concentration. D'Aluisio and Menzel's (2000, p.175) documentation of a robot surgical practice at a hospital in Leipzig describes how the German surgeons have chosen to move the console out of the operating theatre to enable the surgeon's total immersion in the magnified image of the operating field, thus eliminating sources of distraction. Communication with the supplementary surgeon and other members in the team is mediated through microphones. The Leipzig surgeon explained the initiative to distant himself from the patient and the other staff members as follows:

> I'm happy that I don't hear them anymore. Because it's a new way of surgery and you want to be totally immersed in that image. Your brain can only process so much information. If you hear something—the brain has to process it. To concentrate, you try to shut off all those inputs you don't need, which leaves more space for the rest of the information. (2000, p. 175)

In this quotation, a practitioner who is working from the surgical console reflects on the ability to filter out "noise" from a remote location in the hospital. The surgeon wants to be completely immersed in the stereoscopic images provided from the robotic systems. The surgeon goes on to describe the intellectual challenge of adjusting to the multi-dimensional 3D visual tool, a tool that also filters out unnecessary negative stimulus from the operating theatre environment. As Murphy notes, "… focusing on a single signal entails a learned inattention to other noise. Perception always involves disengaging from a broader field of possibilities for the sake of focusing on, isolating, and rendering intelligible a more narrowly delineated set of qualities." (2006, pp. 24–25). Through years of day-to-day practice and experience, physicians become trained at filtering important information from the unimportant, and this involves developing the skill to effectively differentiate the "normal" from the "peculiar" and identify certain patterns in the anatomy during surgery. The surgeons' perception is manifested in the ability to direct their attention to particular details while ignoring others.

2.4.2 Surgical Imaging In Vivo

Thus far we have illustrated how new modes of surgical knowing, visual attention and immersion are situated in surgical practices that are changing from using the apparently restricted 2-dimensional images to more detailed images in 3D stereoscopic robotic surgery. In the final part of the empirical case description, we want to turn to another category of health care professionals in surgery, namely medical illustrators. The connection between touch and vision can also be found in illustrators' facility with new emerging imaging technology. The biggest transition in the knowledge about the body has been the development of imaging in vivo, which takes place in a living organism as opposed to the study of cadavers. When one medical illustrator explained how her clients responded to her work, she highlighted how images can help doctors form the mental models they already have in their heads, based on their years of experience understanding the human body:

> So when they see something illustrated in full-colour in a really nice style, to them that's just, that's just the cat's pajamas. And they always say, and I can't tell you how many doctors that have said, 'that's exactly what it looks like.' But it's not exactly what it looks

like. What I figure it is, I must be hitting on, it's exactly like the image that they've formed in their head 'cause they've done the same thing in their head that I've done graphically, which is remove all the extraneous that's not important, focus in on what is important, ….

For skilled medical illustrators who have worked with surgical illustrations for many years, newly generated 4D images may create both new practical and theoretical knowledge (see Fig. 2.6a, b). One of the interviewed medical illustrators showed a beating heart in a 4D OsiriX reconstruction[4] to one of his colleagues who had worked in the profession for many years; this colleague, who was astonished, commented "… 'the heart doesn't do that' [to which the medical illustrator responded] … well that may be, but this heart did this and here's a movie of it doing it. You think you know what the inside of the beating heart looks like, there's no way to know that". As the quotation suggests, such a transition to visual 4D and displays including functionality, in effect, makes certain unobservable details observable, and thus renders the invisible visible. Mediated multi-dimensional images seem to expand the practitioner's faculty of perceiving in real-time by focusing their attention on hitherto unnoticed aspects.

> …you can do all the dissections you want. But you're seeing in death. … I have a movie of the beating heart where I make everything translucent except for the bolus of blood inside the left ventricle. And you get to see this thing beat …, and … you see a tremendous difference, in which you learn, … that the internal volume of the heart changes much more than the external volume of [the] heart, much more, it's not even close. And you'd never know that from books.

As expressed by the medical illustrators, images previously based on normalized cadaver-based anatomy are now individually rendered in life, and put to work within the surgical theatre. Surgeons themselves discuss the benefits of visualizing hidden anatomy through new imaging modalities, in part reducing risks to patients (Brodke and Randolph 2003). Surgeons use image data to locate the areas of concern prior to surgery as well as use the same images to navigate to the areas of concern during surgery. Figure 2.7a, b features an example of this imaging integration during a focal laser ablation surgery of a tumour of the prostate.

Examples from prostate cancer treatment demonstrate the real-time use of magnetic resonance sequences to create an image of the prostate in a 3D space. As described by health professionals working at Princess Margaret Hospital:

> This 3D image of the prostate and surrounding structures will remain available while the probe of a miniature surgical robot is manipulated percutaneously into the cancer. The miniature surgical robot is strategically placed adjacent to the perineum with the patient in the bore of the magnet. This probe uses image information from the MR machine as a guide for the precise elimination of cancerous cells. The location of the probe is guided with computer software, ensuring precision in the destruction of the area of concern.

The work of the surgeon in these cases is pre-planned and then conducted through the visual environment. These examples of surgical imaging in practice

---

[4] OsiriX® is one of many medical image viewers available for Digital Imaging and Communications in Medicine (DICOM) file types.

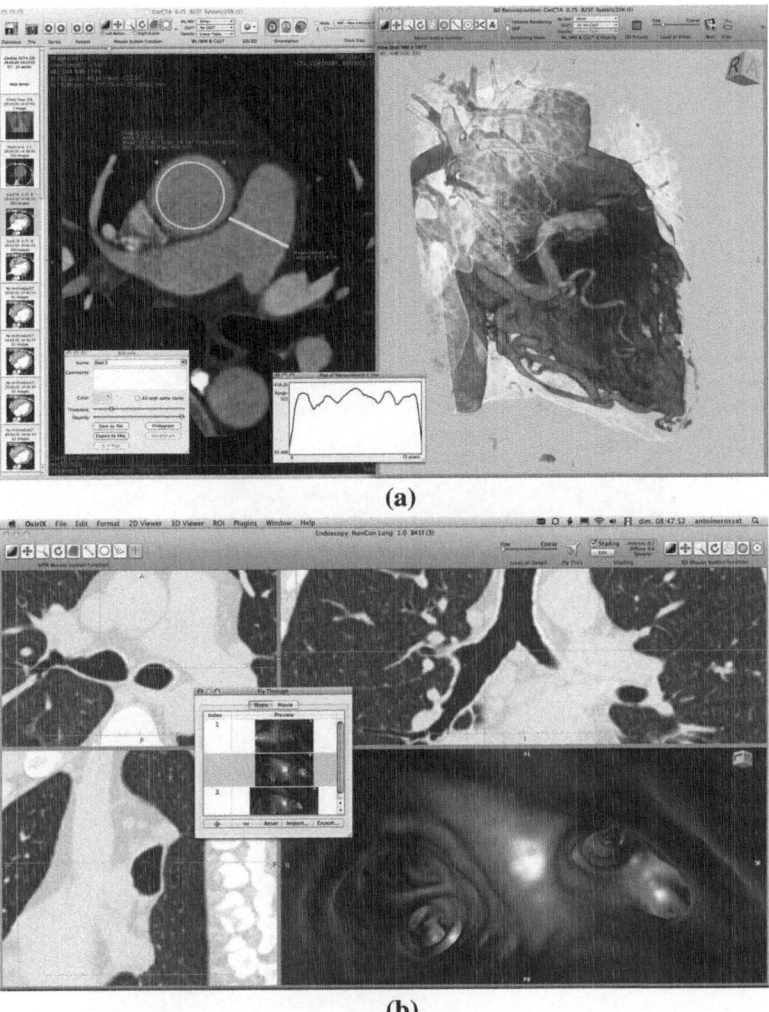

(a)

(b)

Fig. 2.6 a 3D virtual reality of the human heart. A volume renderer such as the OsiriX® software featured here provides a means of working with information based on data captured in the live human body. The 4D and "5D options" (three dimensions, time and functionality) offered by OsiriX® are particularly helpful when examining anatomical relationships over time. Previously "untouchable" activities of the human body, such as the heart beating, can now be explored in life and multiple dimensions. Human vision and image manipulation take the place of touch. © A Rosset, OsiriX **b** The in vivo non-stereoscopic 3-D result of the OsiriX® endoscopy viewer of the human lung. © Antoine Rosset, OsiriX

highlight both the information provided in vivo and the precision provided by the visual. Anatomy that was once hidden to knowledge is newly available to surgical work as it is being done.

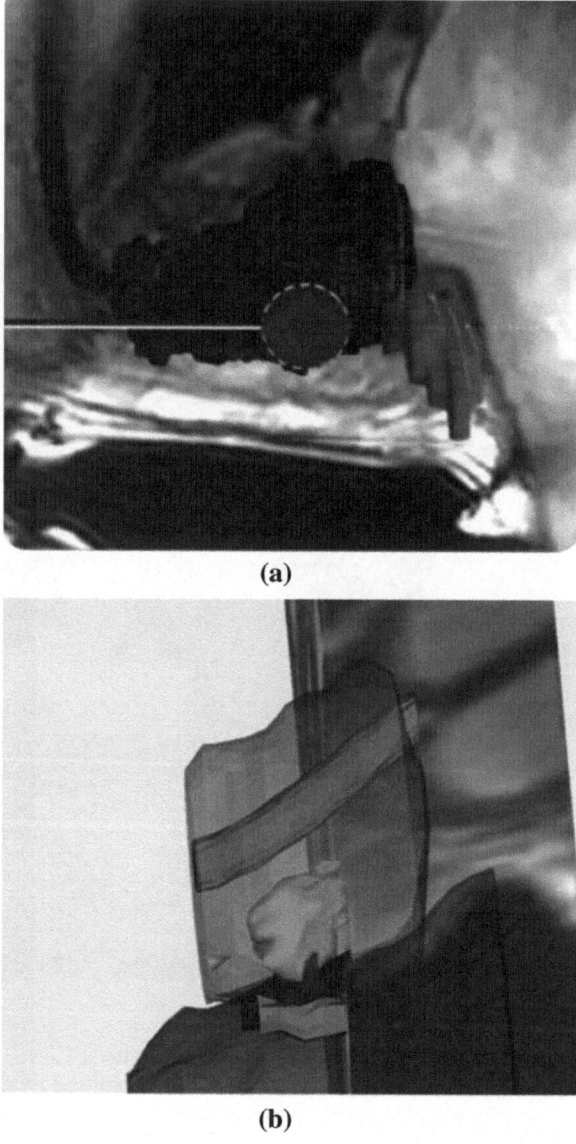

(a)

(b)

Fig. 2.7 a, b Two frames from animated and live footage videos demonstrating focal laser ablation (FLA) therapy procedures of the prostate. Laser heat is used to raise the temperature of the area of concern to a point where the tumour can no longer survive **a** The first frame is a screen capture from an animation which gives a general overview of each of the steps in the FLA procedure. As described by the Prostate Cancer Centre: "… [During the step] when the probe is activated, the cancer and a small margin of surrounding tissue are destroyed. The volume of destruction is visualized in real time and consequently, the margins, or the area around the cancer, are minimized. Blood vessels, nerves and other vital structures are untouched and remain healthy." **b** The second frame is a screen capture from a video that shows MRI image data. The prostate is green–blue, the tumour is blue, the urethra and nerves are yellow, and the area receiving heat from the laser is pink. © The Prostate Centre, Princess Margaret Hospital, University Health Network, Toronto Ontario http://focalprostatecancertherapy.com

2.4.3 Transition in Sensory Focus and Professional Expertise

In robotic surgery, the loss of touch is balanced by remote visual information from the patients. The increased dependency on vision is compensated by the high magnifications possible with new imaging technologies, or to use Ideh's (Ihde 1995) notion 'perception enhancing technologies', which results in surgical precision at scales that surgery based on touch has not able to achieve. These aspects demand special attention to the experience, perception, and embodied knowledge required for in vivo image-mediated surgical procedures.

Based on the rich empirical data from their use, it is clear that emerging visual technologies, either in the form of three-dimensional (3D) stereoscopic images from high-resolution (HD) cameras or four-dimensional (4D) images, such as those generated by the OsiriX® system, can help focus attention on very small details. By enlarging and enhancing the surgeon's visual capacity, this sophisticated technology makes numerous things perceptible but renders other things imperceptible. Surgeons can push a button on the console and pan the 3D camera to view the periphery, which provides them with a curved view (a so called "curved arcing view"). This image is a representation, or an indirect mediated view. During surgery, surgeons need to be able to evaluate the situation in the periphery outside the narrow working area. Most of today's vision systems do not provide surgeons with the entire peripheral view, which is available in traditional surgery, thus limiting their ability to observe the field from an angle other than a direct one. This limitation is especially salient in laparoscopic two-dimensional (2D) vision systems because this type of surgery does not generate a curved view but instead creates a flat view. Based on the detailed accounts of surgeons, however, the advantage gained by the new enhanced three-dimensional vision and heightened perception clearly outweighs any of the drawbacks of imperceptibility that may be related to the tunnel vision inherent in this indirect vision.

It is important to note that the surgeon's work still relies heavily on expertise and tacit knowledge; however, human experience and vision *per se* may not be enough for the surgeon to see and discern all the important and relevant anatomical structures needed to treat a patient successfully. Therefore, knowledge and mediated vision go hand in hand. The human actor is given new visual capabilities in the enactment with a series of assemblages that pertain to certain material qualities. We introduce the concept of "sensory awareness" (McLuhan 1964) to further discuss the fundamental transition involved in the interaction between technology and surgeons from a traditional unaided vision to a "multi-dimensional visual touch".

The theory of "sensory awareness" is central to McLuhan's (1964) philosophy, which portrays human existence in an increasingly technological world. This study considers the experiences from medical practices employing sophisticated visualisation technology. The concept of "sensory awareness" in this study explicitly emphasises the mutually enhancing and complementary characteristics of surgeons and their tools (both physical and mental) that assist in accomplishing tasks and activities. That is to say, robot technology applied in a medical setting supports and extends a surgeon's capabilities and sensory feedback. McLuhan (1964) maintains that the positive effect of putting a new medium or technology to use is that it generally expands people's inherent senses. This, in turn, enables new ways of experiencing the world. Paradoxically, the negative effect is that any artificial extension of one sense simultaneously moves another sense to the background (i.e., an "amputation", in McLuhan's terminology). This dual effect is a common characteristic of most modern technologies, and it disproportionately unbalances our senses. Hence, innovative robot technology in surgery, for example, liberates former constraints, such as the limited human vision and lack of precise hand movements. At the same time, new robotic procedures create new constraints; they exclude abilities such as the sense of touch through the surgeon's fingers (often called force or haptic feedback) as well as temperature, viscosity and other characteristics that provide the surgeon with significant information.

"Sensing is believing" is the articulation of a theory that may help explain why most surgeons in this study exhibit frustration regarding the loss of physical sensation. Physical feedback for surgeons is a "situational feedback" mechanism or a reflective practice in action in which surgeons continuously "let the situation talk back" (Schön 1983). According to Donald Schön, practitioners may take the role of the artist in the "situational backtalk" and enter into a "reflective conversation with the materials of the situation". By physically experiencing the procedure and interacting with the patient in traditional open surgery (for example, by touching the internal structures and feeling the resistance), surgeons are actually engaged in a physical form of dialogue with the patient's body and organs (Hannaford 1996). Daston (2008) describes how insight and learned experience among individuals is developed in a type of "disciplination of the gaze" by focusing on what is important, which is an ability that is acquired through years of long-term training and day-to-day work in the OR (see also Goodwin (1994) seminal work on "professional vision").

Grasseni (2007) offers the related concept of "skilled visions" where multisensoriality, skilled movement, and changes in points of view are important for accomplishing objectives (see also Pink 2009, p. 13). Clearly, the surgeon's vision (or "the surgical gaze") involves the ability to inspect a multitude of visual representations of the anatomy that are captured and enhanced by the technologies described above.

2.5 Regimes of Visual Attention: Perceptibility and Imperceptibility

Perceptibility and imperceptibility are concepts that have been extensively discussed and empirically scrutinised in various management science settings (also known as business studies or business administration), particularly in studies drawing on related work in psychology (Bruner 1957; Tversky 1972) and in the field commonly known as organisation theory (Beyer et al. 1997; Louise and Sutton 1991). In this line of research, Dearborn and Simon's (1958) work on managers' information management and decision-making is especially significant. More recently, Beyer et al. (1997) re-examined Dearborn and Simon's work on "selective perception" and found that cognitive labour can also direct attention away from certain information aggregates. Beyer et al. (1997) describe how professionals apply what they call "selective imperceptions", referring to people's occasional failure to perceive certain information.

Perceptibility and imperceptibility, however, are not two isolated dimensions of intellectual work and information handling capacity confined merely to intellectual (mentalistic) phenomena. Some organisational theorists have extended these terms beyond the mentalistic level towards human awareness and their connection to the senses. For example, Tsoukas and Chia (2002, p. 571) draw on Bergson's work The Creative Mind (published in 1946) to show that a key to making sense of the emergence of change (flux) and complexity in contemporary social and organisational settings is not necessarily an intellectual understanding (reflection), but rather the result of engaging with the sensory world. Thus, they argue "… turn toward sensation; bring yourself in touch with reality through intuition; get to know it from within or, to use Wittgenstein's (1958) famous aphorism, "don't think, but look" (para. 66). Only a direct perception of reality will enable one to get a glimpse of its most salient characteristics".

Following Tsoukas and Chai (2002, p. 571), human understanding and perception are closely linked to the use of the senses and are unfolding processes (what they refer to as movements) in which not necessarily reflection-based knowledge but rather "direct knowledge" of the constantly changing state of affairs is gained.

Clearly, new visual technologies are changing what can and cannot be detected by the senses in the new work regimes we describe. For example, one practitioner described how he literally could put his finger on the edge of a beating heart, which was displayed on a 4D image projection. By seeing the heart's movements, he was also able to observe previously unknown variations in a patient's anatomy, in this case, the internal volume of a beating heart ("the left lateral margin"), which the 4D OsiriX® reconstruction rendered visible. However, Tsoukas and Chai note that human perception is inherently limited because there will always be small variations that the sensory apparatus cannot detect. This fact is also true for visual technologies. Therefore, it becomes important to reflect on what reveals the imperceptible in the use of image-guided technologies. This observation is consonant with Murphy's point that "Seeing necessitates the designation of the unseeable, knowing the unknowable" (2006, p. 9).

More recent research shows that perceptibility and imperceptibility are both tightly interwoven with social practices, material cultures and complex technological infrastructures situated in wider socio-cultural environments. Along these lines and in Murphy's (2006, p. 24) terms, perception is thus distinguished

.... by historically specific modes of paying attention, which always necessitate strategic suspensions of perception. Perception involves historically produced disengagements from a broader field of bombardments for the sake of concentrating on and rendering intelligible a more narrowly differentiated set of phenomena.

Haraway (1991) here reminds us that there are no ahistorical and neutral images and no impartial photographs in scientific imaging practices, only specific viewpoints, or what she calls "visual possibilities".

> The 'eyes' made available in modern technological sciences shatter any idea of passive vision; these prosthetic devices show us that all eyes, including our own organic ones, are active perceptual systems, building in translations and specific ways of seeing, that is, ways of life. There is no unmediated photograph or passive camera obscura in scientific accounts of bodies and machines; there are only highly specific visual possibilities, each with a wonderfully detailed, active, partial way of organizing worlds (1991, p. 175).

Some scholars attempt to disentangle and historicise dominant domains of perceptibility. Murphy (2006) introduced the concept of "regimes of perceptibility and imperceptibility", which is

> ... the regular and sedimented contours of perception and imperceptions produced within a disciplinary or epistemological tradition. Regimes of perceptibility are about more than just what we can see. As regimes, they were often understood by the historical actors employing them as natural or inevitable outcomes of social and technical arrangements. Produced by assemblages that are anchored in material culture, regimes of perceptibility establish what phenomena become perceptible and thus what phenomena come into being for us, giving objects boundaries and imbuing them with qualities. Regimes of perceptibility populate our world with some objects and not others, and they allow certain actions to be performed on those objects. (Murphy 2006, pp. 24–25)

Although this elaboration of "regimes of perceptibility" concerns ontological matters, also relevant is how regimes are embedded in the competing material, technological, and institutional cultures that affect epistemic practices. Regimes of perceptibility and imperceptibility are always situated in certain space–time segments and are therefore limited to particular materialities and physical settings.[5] The forms of such regimes make certain socio-political, institutional and historical circumstances possible, Murphy argues. If we want to understand what is actually happening in image-guided medicine, we need to understand the dominant social ontology in epistemic practices. We also need to include the wider historical and material conditions in which dominant social ontologies of medical work are entrenched. Our initial premise was that

---

[5] Murphy's (2006) study accounts for how office personnel were exposed to dangerous chemicals in their work environments. She describes how there were simultaneous notions of "sickness" and "wellness" in the history of the ontology of chemical exposure. At a certain moment in time, what was considered imperceptible in a sick building later became re-defined and eventually known as "sick building syndrome". This ontological shift occurred because a new expertise of a different type, with a new set of apparatuses, entered the scene and managed to capture "sickness" in the realm of the perceptible. In this line of reasoning, what constitutes a certain ontology regime is bound to local conditions and situates knowledge at a micro- or meso-level (such as in the context of buildings and surgical interfaces) but is at the same time also bound to wider historical and material conditions. The attractiveness of the phrase "regimes of perceptibility and imperceptibility" is that it appreciates the tension between the seeable and invisible, the knowable and unknowable, and the "existent" and "nonexistent" in certain historical and material conditions.

where surgeons' movements and the uses of senses change with new imaging technologies, so must their perceptual approaches and their embodied understandings of surgery itself.

2.5.1 Vision is Not An Isolated Given

Vision interacts with the other senses as part of the community of practice to which surgeons belong. This line of analysis has two important implications. First, images do not speak for themselves. Styhre (2010b) maintains that professional vision is never isolated but is rather manifested in shared professional norms and certain ways of thought in an organisational setting. Therefore, professional vision is always under the influence of these norms, as "... this gaze is never wholly self-enclosed but is instead always under the threat of disintegrating or falling apart. That is why specific thought collectives must maintain their authority and jurisdiction over certain 'ways of seeing'" (Styhre 2010b, pp. 72–73).

The production, analysis, and use of medical images are situated in a cultural context in what Foucault (1973) has described as "regimes of truth", which temporarily stabilise and institutionalise the borders between what is thinkable and unthinkable and what is reasonable and unreasonable in a medical setting. What is considered seeable or unseeable within a community of professionals, such as a community of physicians is, according to Foucault's line of reasoning, tightly coupled to power and authority.

While images produced in medicine (and in science) might appear objective and universal, only certain viewpoints are honoured, while others are overlooked. (Joyce 2005) Timmermans discusses (2008, p.170), on the one hand, a form of "disciplinary objectivity" in professional activities, but on the other hand is, of course, a "less disciplined objectivity". In professional practices, there are always openings for deviances, anomalies and differences in interpreting images. In the quest to divert from the tight disciplinary power of the thinkable and reasonable, new insights may arise and new knowledge and embodied knowing developed.

2.6 Touching New Visual Worlds: Discovering New Knowledge

> There are times in life when the question of knowing if one can think differently than one thinks, and perceive differently than one sees, is absolutely necessary if one is to go on looking and reflecting at all. Michel Foucault, The Use of Pleasure

The distinction between "medicine as art" and "medicine as science" is still very much alive today. Our argument, however, is that the differences between the two may soon abate and that the two notions of medicine in fact are inseparable and increasingly interlinked with technology. Hence, robotic surgery is a practice in which science, technology and art are combined. The experience and maturity, which some call artistic "intuition" (Cohn 2007, p. 93) of surgery are maintained in parallel with technological confidence and scientific certainty.

Knowledge is dependent on and embodied in the individual and, as von Krogh et al. suggest, "Where you stand or what you know determines what you see or what you choose to be relevant" (1994, p. 58). "Visual knowledge" (Cohn 2007) and "observation" thus become closely related. Haraway (2000, p. 160) argues, "[S]cientific knowledge is about witnessing. That is what the experimental method is about, the fact of being there". In the intensified blending of science, medicine, and technology, multi-dimensional imaging instruments function partly as ordering devices. The shift in several scientific visual regimes is actually beginning to reshape medical practices as well as other domains in the natural sciences. This shift becomes especially salient in how multi-dimensional images *per se* become perceptible as scientific facts, as a result of new modes of organising and ordering of new data, information, and knowledge. While some aspects are made visible by the new forms of multi-dimensional representations, equally important is to question the limits of new image-based knowledge. As Murphy (2006, p. 91) notes, "To create knowledge means to create a tunnel where other things are not chosen". Following Murphy, this means to ask what falls outside of the knowledge being produced under the present circumstances, which highlights the limits of regimes of perceptibility and their boundaries to the imperceptible.

It is important to study this shift in epistemic practices because imaging in the making also changes everyday conceptions of scientific enterprises. These new imaging practices represent a new form of art and science in modern medicine, and to use Nonaka and Takeuchi's (1995) notion, robotic surgery "re-creates the professional environment". It is still an art because image-guided robotic surgery and scientific imaging involve professional problem solving, expertise and social creativity because every patient or case is unique. It is still a science-based practice because it relies on the proper use of medical knowledge, which is based on application of best practices in the treatment of patients and which adds value to the health care system.

The particular shift we have discussed focuses on the replacement of human touch by 3-dimensional visual touch. Remote handling technologies are able to facilitate such an artificial metallic touch. Working through 3-dimensional images changes the type of surgical work carried out and the sensory relationships required and understood as knowledge. The shift in authority from touch to visual sensation in modern surgery is one we find increasingly predominant in contemporary culture and society in general. Interestingly, we see that scholars working in several scientific domains recently have begun to use 3D as well as 4D and 5D visualisation as a powerful instrument for innovative knowledge production.

Knowledge production is found in the way scientists interact with new tools. In an ethnographic study of human encounters with imaging technology, Morana Alac (2008) studied lab technicians' interactions with functional magnetic resonance imaging (fMRI) data. Alac demonstrates how seeing digital images "involves the hands as well as the eyes" (p. 505). Alac watches neuroscientists use gestures as an interface between their bodies and the technologies representing fMRI, manipulating digital displays and gesturing to make sense of their experimental data. In acknowledging the embodied process of 'seeing' fMRI, Alac demonstrates that "reading digital images enables them [neuroscientists] to re-enter a world of culturally meaningful embodied actions" (p. 504). These "gestural engagements" meet at the junction between the digital world and the world of embodied action (p. 484).

When images become tools, they also include their own "gestural engagements." Daston and Galison (2007), write that "Images become tools like other tools, part of the apparatus—more like the computer screen that shows the workings of a distantly controlled robotic manipulation in remote surgery…" (p. 414). These practices meet at the junction between the digital world and the world of embodied action. Surgical instrumentation participates in adjusting how the surgeon navigates his or her material world, requiring a variety of gestures and directing surgical practices to stabilise human worlds. People's actions might just as well be based on relationships with objects in the world as routine social activity (Schatzki et al. 2001, p. 19).

When images mediate the connection between the surgeon and a patient's body, these actions necessarily change the way the body is understood (Beaulieu 2000; Waldby 2000). Understanding the world is accomplished through explicit and tacit knowledge, and part of this tacit knowledge must involve changes in sensorial focus and understandings that are a result of this focus. The surgeons interviewed in this study confirmed the challenges and triumphs of dealing with new imaging technologies as a change in their habitual understandings.

Interestingly, if applied appropriately, the very same complex imaging technology also leads to new forms of professional knowledge production. What we refer to as "multi-dimensional visual touch" currently serves as a key component in the development of professional surgical expertise. This chapter advances the idea that robotics and imaging devices in surgery are not only technological breakthroughs but also enable professionals to acquire new knowledge based on detailed 3D, 4D and 5D images. As Nancy Nersessian explains in "Creating Scientific Concepts", "contrary to the popular image of science, … conceptual innovation … emerges from lengthy, organic processes and requires a combination of inherited and environmental conditions" (2008, p. ix). The imaging changes that occur in surgical practice are part of a larger context.

Addressing the initial distinction between "medicine as art" and "medicine as science", it is useful to keep in mind that 3D technology does not result in creativity, innovation and new knowledge *per se* if it simply maintains the old ways of doing things. If 3D images merely reproduce known facts and representations of the world, just as artists from time to time reproduce and duplicate paintings and other forms of art, there is no real genuine incentive for change and innovation. However, if 3D, 4D and 5D images reveal something new and change the way people see the world, there is a foundation on which to develop new knowledge and understanding. The shift to either 3D, 4D or 5D visual technology still has professional expertise at the centre of attention and relates to Webber's point that, "In the end, the location of the new economy is not in the technology or in the microchip or the global telecommunications network. It is in the human mind." (Webber 1993, p. 27).

In the case of 3D technology assisting surgeons in image-guided robotic surgery, 3D visual feedback is a sophisticated tool that incorporates certain skills in the configuration and distribution of image data to the surgeon. Our findings prove the fact that images must be processed and endowed with purpose, as well as a relevance that is ordered, interpreted, and analysed by professional surgeons. While a robot has the ability to collect and store data, it cannot analyse, interpret or act on the raw data generated from 3D imaging systems. The surgical robot in this case is not an "innovator" or a creative entity; it is a sophisticated tool. The knowledge eventually attained is embodied in a medical expert, and knowledge creation is characterised according to its relative tacitness and social embeddedness. As the nature of surgery changes, so will the demands for usable surgical expertise in the future. Our research suggests that the role of the surgeon has changed and will continue to change over the coming decades by scientific and technological breakthroughs in medical care. In light of the progression of modern high-tech health care, robotics is regarded both as a threat and an opportunity for contemporary professionals.

Based on an in-depth investigation of robotic surgery, we suggest that the phenomenon of 3D imaging technology affects how professionals experience the world and the capacity for 3D technology to guide human perception and action. While we focus on a limited case study of how vision is mediated by 3D technology in surgery, we also generalise this observation to the entire scientific domain because 3D, 4D and 5D imaging technology is changing the way science is conducted.

Multi-dimensional visual interaction implies a new method to perform work tasks. A wide variety of applications emerging from 3D imaging are starting to make a significant impact on key scientific progress in anthropology, archaeology, and medicine. The social motivation to innovate and adapt 3D image technology in science is related to the desire to improve social well-being as well as to advance knowledge. Anthropologists are now using high-resolution 3D videos as a conservation technique of artefacts (Scopigno et al. 2011) as well as for reconstructing ancient tombs and landscapes (Bruno 2010). Three-dimensional scanning data also provide scholars with a novel opportunity to store long-term digital archives of important cultural artefacts for future generations. For example, archaeologists have created a digitised 3D model in colour of Michelangelo's 5-metre statue of David. (Levoy et al. 2000) An article in Science recently reported that scholars have started using high-speed 3D video microscopy in medical experiments to better understand the underlying processes involved in viral transfer events, resulting in new knowledge that may help to develop future vaccines (Hübner et al. 2009). While the most recent usage of 3D image devices promise to revolutionise scientific practice in certain domains, much of the current knowledge about the emerging 3D applications remains based on computational modelling and 3D models of virtual places. The concept of 3D imaging in real-life may be moving from a potentially disruptive technology in science to crucial practice in other societal domains, such as entertainment, advertising, and education. This presents an area for future research.

We describe how the ability to see in depth in the real 3D world may also have a significant impact on other sectors and businesses in society. In endeavouring to attain the knowledge attributed to images, in combination with the precision images afford, gestural worlds shift and new possibilities arise.

2.7 Conclusion: Seeing and Knowing in Multi-Sensorial Worlds

As the surgeons' movements and use of senses are changed by the new imaging technologies, so must the surgeon's perceptual approaches and embodied understandings and knowledge of surgery change. Exploring the expansion of vision therefore contributes to an epistemological and ontological reconsideration.

Transitions in surgical practice provide an intimate view of the reconciliation of vision and touch. We propose the notion "visual touch", a conceptual middle ground between touch and vision, as a basis for future research in exploring contemporary institutional regimes of image-based work. "Visual touch" is both the process of reconciling the senses (human and artificial) and the end result of this sensorial union. In the words of the surgeons and the illustrators interviewed, there is a longing for what is yet to be known and done.

In our view, practices of seeing and knowing in multi-sensorial worlds are coupled to creative processes of serendipity in medical and scientific knowledge. When individuals are touching new visual worlds in real-time 3D, 4D or "5D" imaging, they are also able to discover unexpected knowledge and gain new insight. Changes in work practices sometimes make it impossible to return to previous times. It is a form of path dependency, where the decisions made in the past influence what we do in the present. Yet in the move to an image-mediated surgical experience, the multisensorial remains a topic of conversation—will surgeons continue to demand a more focused visual experience and deny the need for human touch and audio feedback, which some surgeons appear to appreciate doing without?

Another question that arises is whether it is possible for the surgical community to return to practices that do not emphasise vision. Indeed, it is possible to envision a different path where in the future, robotic technology will provide multisensory representations of the surroundings.

Institutional innovations consist of gradual adjustments to how we live in the world and may result in unplanned consequences (Pantzar and Shove 2010). Scholars who study organisational innovation see it as a continuous process of creation and evolution in what people do and consider acceptable behaviour. The transitioning sensory requirements of surgeons are part of a changing professional knowledge-based practice that is path-dependent. To obtain a more balanced picture of the future implications of multi-dimensional imaging technologies in robotic surgery and in other medical and scientific practices, these applications should be continually and thoroughly evaluated. This evaluation is not only to scientifically confirm the promised benefits of surgical processes but also to understand what is taken for granted in the world and how new and unexpected knowledge is discovered.

References

Alac, M. (2008). Working with brain scans: Digital images and gestural interaction in fMRI laboratory. *Social Studies of Science, 38*(4), 483–508.

Bal, M. (2003). Visual essentialism and the object of visual culture. *Journal of Visual Culture, 1*, 5–32.

Barley, S. R., & Kunda, G. (2001). Bringing work back in. *Organization Science, 12*(1), 76–95.

Beaulieu, A. (2000). *The space inside the skull: Digital representations, brain mapping, and cognitive neuroscience in the decade of the brain*. Doctoral dissertation, University of Amsterdam.

Beaulieu, A. (2003). Brains, maps and the new territory of psychology. *Theory & Psychology, 13*(4), 561–568.

Bergson, H. (1908/1988). *Matter and memory*. New York: Zone Books.

Beyer, J. M., Prithviraj, C., Glick, G. W., & Pulise, D. (1997). The selective perception of managers revisited. *Academy of Management Journal, 40*(3), 716–737.

Bicker, R., Burn, K., Hu, Z., Pongean, W., & Bashir, A. (2004). *The early development of remote tele-manipulation systems. Proceedings International Symposium on History of Machines and Mechanisms*. New York: Kluwer Academic Publishers.

Blackler, F. (1995). Knowledge, knowledge work and organizations: An overview and interpretation. *Organization Studies, 6*, 1021–1046.

Bourdieu, P. (1977). *Outline of a theory of practice*. New York: Cambridge University Press.

Brodke, D., & Randolph, G. (2003). Image guidance for spinal surgery. *Operative techniques in orthopaedics, 3*, 152–158.

Bruner, J. S. (1957). On perceptual readiness. *Psychology Review, 64*, 123–152.

Bruno, F., Bruno, S., De Sensi, G., Luchi, M-L., Mancuso, S., & Muzzupappa, M.(2010). From 3D reconstruction to virtual reality: A complete methodology for digital archaeological exhibition. *Journal of Cultural Heritage, 11*, 42–49.

Burri, R. V., & Dumit, J. (2008). Social studies of scientific imaging and visualization. In E. J. Hackett, O. Amsterdamska, M. Lynch, & J. Wajcman (Eds.), *The handbook of science and technology studies* (3rd ed., pp. 297–317). Cambridge, MA: The MIT Press.

Bynum, W. F., & Porter, R. (Eds.). (1993). *Companion encyclopedia of the history of medicine*. London: Routledge.

Cartwright, F. F. (1967). *The development of modern surgery*. London: Arthur Baker.

Cepolina, F., Challacombe, B., & Michelini, R. C. (2005). Trends in robotic surgery. *Journal of Endourology, 19*(8), 940–950.

Classen, C. (1993). *Worlds of sense: Exploring the senses in history and across cultures*. London: Routledge.

Cohn, S. (2007). Seeing and drawing: The role of play in medical imaging. In C. Grasseni (Ed.), *Skilled visions: Between apprenticeship and standards* (pp. 91–105). New York: Berghahn Books.

Collins, H. (2010). *Tacit and explicit knowledge*. Chicago: The University of Chicago Press.

Crosby, R. W., & Cody, J. (1991). *The man who put art into medicine*. New York: Springer.

Daston, L. (2008). On scientific observation. *Isis, 99*, 97–110.

Daston, L., & Galison, P. (2007). *Objectivity*. Brooklyn, NY: Zone Books.

Davenport, T. H., & Pruskak, L. (1998). *Working knowledge: How organizations manage what they know*. Boston: Harvard Business School Press.

Davidson, J. M. (1916). *Localization by x-rays and stereoscopy*. New York: Paul B. Hoeber.

Dearborn, D. C., & Simon, H. A. (1958). Selective perception: A note on the departmental identification of executives, *Sociometry, June*: 140–148.

Engström, T., & Selenger, E. (Eds.). (2009). *Rethinking theories and practices of imaging*. London: Palgrave Macmillan.

Feld, S. (2005). Places sensed, senses placed: Toward a sensuous epistemology of environments. In D. Howes (Ed.), *Empire of the senses* (pp. 179–191). Oxford: Berg.

Freeman, C. (1994). The economics of technical change. *Cambridge Journal of Economics, 18*(5), 463–514.

Foucault, M. (1973). *The birth of the clinic: An archaeology of medical perception.* London: Routledge.

Galison, P. (1997). *Image and logic: A material culture of microphysics.* Chicago: University of Chicago Press.

Geertz, C. (1983). *The interpretation of cultures.* New York: Basic Books.

Getty, D. J., & Green, P. J. (2007). Clinical applications for stereoscopic 3-D displays. *Journal of the Society for Information Display, 6*, 377–384.

Goodwin, C. (1994). Professional vision. *American Anthropologist, 96*(3), 606–633.

Grasseni, C. (2007). *Skilled visions: Between apprenticeship and standards.* New York: Berghahn Books.

Göranzon, B., Gullers, P., Mäkilä, K., et al. (1987). *Datorn som verktyg.* Studentlitteratur: Lund.

Hannaford, B. (1996). Feeling is believing: Haptics and telerobotics technology. In K. Goldberg (Ed.), *The robot in the garden, telerobotics and telepistomology on the internet* (pp. 246–275). Cambridge, MA: MIT Press.

Haraway, D. J. (1991). Situated knowledges: The science question in feminism and the privilege of partial perspective. In M. Lederman & I. Bartsch (Eds.), *The gender and science reader* (pp. 169–188). London: Routledge.

Haraway, D. J. (2000). *How like a leaf: An interview with Thyrza Nichols Goodeve.* New York: Routledge.

Harding-Rains, A. J. (1977). *Joseph Lister and antisepsis.* Hove Sussex: Priory Press.

Hawkins, R., & Verhoest, P. (2002). A transaction structure approach to assessing the dynamics and impacts of business-to-business electronic commerce, *Journal of Computer-Mediated Communication, 7*(3).

Held, R. T., & Hui, T. T. (2011). A guide to stereoscopic 3D displays in medicine. *Academic Radiology, 8*, 1035–1048.

Henderson, K. (1999). *On line and on paper: Visual representations, visual culture and computer graphics in design engineering.* Cambridge, MA: MIT Press.

Hofmeister, J., Frank, T., Cuschieri, A., & Wade, N. J. (2001). Perceptual aspects of two-dimensional and stereoscopic display techniques in endoscopic surgery: Review and current problems. *Surgical Innovation, 8*(1), 12–24.

Holtzmann-Kevles, B. (1997). *Naked to the bone: Medical imaging in the twentieth century.* New Jersey: Rutgers University Press.

Howes, D. (2005). Skinscapes: Embodiment, culture and environment. In C. Classen (Ed.), *The book of touch.* Oxford: Berg.

Hübner, W., McNerney, G. P., Chen, P., et al. (2009). Quantitative 3D video microscopy of HIV transfer synapses. *Science, 27* March: 1743–1747.

Ihde, D. (1995). Image technologies and traditional culture. In A. Feenberg (Ed.), *Technology and the politics of knowledge.* Bloomington: Indiana University Press.

Jastrow, J. (1936). *The story of human error.* New York: Ayer Company Publishers.

Joyce, K. (2005). Appealing images: Magnetic resonance imaging and the production of authoritative knowledge. *Social Studies of Science, 35*(3), 437–462.

Kincaid, D. L. (2004). From innovation to social norm: Bounded normative influence. *Journal of Health Communication, 9*, 37–57.

Knorr Cetina, K. (2001). Objectual practice. In T. Schatzki, K. Knorr Cetina, & E. Von Savigney (Eds.), *The practice turn in contemporary theory.* London: Routledge.

Knorr Cetina, K. (1999). *Epistemic cultures: How the sciences make knowledge.* Cambridge, MA: Harvard University Press.

Landau, J., Groscurth, C. R., Wright, L., & Condit, C. M. (2009). Visualizing nanotechnology: The impact of visual images on lay American audience associations with nanotechnology. *Public Understanding of Science, 18*(3), 325–337.

Latour, B. (1990). Visualisation and cognition: Drawing things together. In M. Lynch & S. Woolgar (Eds.), *Representation in scientific practice* (pp. 19–68). Cambridge, MA: MIT Press.

Lee, S. L., Huntbatch, A., Pratt, P., Lerotic, M., & Yang, G. Z. (2010). In vivo and in situ image guidance and modeling in robotic assisted surgery. *Journal of Mechanical Engineering Science, 224*, 1421–1434.

Levoy, M., Pulli, K., Curless, B., et al. (2000). *The digital Michelangelo project: 3D scanning of large statues* (pp. 131–144). July: Proceedings of ACM SIGGRAPH.

Louise, M. R., & Sutton, R. I. (1991). Switching cognitive gears: From habits of mind to action thinking. *Human Relations, 44*, 55–61.

Marchessault, J., & Sawchuk, K. (2000). *Wild science: Reading feminism, medicine, and the media*. London: Routledge.

Marescaux, J., & Soler, L. (2004). Image-guided robotic surgery. *Seminars in Laparoscopic Surgery, 11*(2), 113–122.

McLuhan, M. (1964). *Understanding media: The extensions of man*. Cambridge, MA: MIT Press.

Menzel, P., & d'Aluisio, D. (2000). *Robo sapiens: Evolution of a new species*. Cambridge, MA: MIT Press.

Merleau-Ponty, M. (1962). *Phenomenology of perception*. London: Routledge.

Mol, A. M. (2002). *The body multiple: Ontology in medical practice*. Durham: Duke University Press.

Morton, R. (1989). Fundamentals of stereophotography in medicine. *Journal of Audiovisual Media in Medicine, 12*, 11–14.

Mumford, L. (1934). *Technics and civilization*. London: SAGE.

Mumford, L. (1952). *Arts and technics*. New York: Columbia University Press.

Murphy, M. (2006). *Sick building syndrome and the problem of uncertainty: Environmental politics, technoscience, and women workers*. Durham: Duke University Press.

Myers, N. (2008). Molecular embodiments and the body-work of modelling in protein crystallography. *Social Studies of Science, 38*(2), 163–199.

Nersessian, N. J. (2008). *Creating scientific concepts*. Cambridge, MA: MIT Press.

Newell, F., & Shams, L. (2007). New insights into multisensory perception. *Perception, 36*, 1415–1418.

Nonaka, I., & Takeuchi, H. (1995). *The knowledge creating company: How Japanese companies create the dynamics of innovation*. New York: Oxford University Press.

OECD. (1996). *Technology, productivity and job creation*. Vol. 2 Analytical report, Paris

OECD. (1994). *The OECD jobs study—facts, analysis, strategies*, Paris.

Oleynikov, D., Rentschler, M. E., Dumpert, J., Platt, S., & Farritor, S. M. (2005). In vivo robotic laparoscopy. *Surgical Innovation, 2*, 177–181.

Oldfield, P., & Landon, R. (2006). *Ars medica medical illustration through the ages: An exhibition to commemorate the seventieth anniversary of the founding of associated medical services*. Toronto: University of Toronto Library.

Pantzar, M., & Shove, E. (2010). Understanding innovation in practice: A discussion of the production and re-production of Nordic walking. *Technology Analysis and Strategic Management, 4*, 447–461.

Patel, A. A., Whang, P. G., & Vaccaro, A. R. (2008). Overview of computer-assisted image-guided surgery of the spine. *Seminars in Spine Surgery, 20*, 186–194.

Paterson, M. (2005). Digital touch. In C. Classen (Ed.), *The book of touch* (pp. 431–436). Oxford: Berg.

Pedersen, J. S., & Dobbin, F. (1997). The social invention of collective actors: On the rise of the organization. *American Behavioral Scientist, 40*(4), 431–443.

Pink, S. (2009). *Doing sensory ethnography*. London: SAGE.

Polanyi, M. (1967/2009). *The tacit dimension*. Chicago: The University of Chicago Press.

Roberts, K. B., & Tomlinson, J. D. W. (1992). *The fabric of the body. European traditions of anatomical illustration*. Oxford: Clarendon Press.

Rogers, E. M. (2003). *Diffusion of innovations* (5th ed). New York: Free Press.

Rosenberger, R. (2011). A case study in the applied philosophy of imaging: The synaptic vesicle debate. *Science, Technology and Human Values, 36*(1), 6–31.

Schatzki, T., Knorr Cetina, K., & von Savigny, E. (2001). *The practice turn in contemporary theory*. London: Routledge.

Schön, D. (1983). *The reflective practitioner*. New York: Basic Books.

Scopigno, R., Callieri, M., Cignoni, P., et al. (2011). 3D models for cultural heritage: Beyond plain visualization. *Computer, 44*(7), 48–55.

Shams, L., Kamitani, Y., & Shimojo, S. (2000). What you see is what you hear. *Nature, 408*, 788.

Speich, J., & Rosen, J. (2004). *Medical robotics, encyclopedia of biomaterials and biomedical engineering*. New York: Marcel Dekker Inc.

Styhre, A. (2010a). Organizing technologies of vision: Making the invisible visible in media-laden observations. *Information and Organization, 20*, 64–78.

Styhre, A. (2010b). *Visual culture in organizations*. New York: Taylor & Francis.

Sullivan, J. T. (1996). Surgery before anesthesia. *American Society of Anesthesiologists, 60*(9), 8–10.

Timmermans, S. (2008). Professions and their work: Do market shelters protect professional interests? *Work and Occupations, 35*(2), 164–188.

Tornatzky, L., & Fleischer, M. (1990). *The processes of technological innovation*. New York: Lexington Books.

Tsafrir, J., & Ohry, A. (2001). Medical illustration: From caves to cyberspace. *Health Information and Libraries Journal, 18*(2), 99–109.

Tsoukas, H., & Chia, R. (2002). On organizational becoming: Rethinking organizational change. *Organization Science, 13*(5), 567–582.

Tversky, A. (1972). Elimination of aspects: A theory of choice. *Psychology Review, 79*, 281–299.

Vertut, J., & Coiffet, P. H. (1985). *Teleoperation and robotics: Application and technology*. London: Kogan Page.

Waldby, C. (2000). The visible human project: Data into flesh, flesh into data. In J. Marchessault & K. Sawchuk (Eds.), *Wild science: Reading feminism, medicine and the media*. London: Routledge.

Wasen, K. (2010). Replacement of highly educated surgical assistants by robot technology in working life: Paradigm shift in the service sector. *International Journal of Social Robotics, 2*(4), 431–438. doi:10.1007/s12369-010-0062-y.

Webber, A. (1993). What's so new about the new economy? *Harvard Business Review, Jan–Feb*, 24–32.

Wejnert, B. (2002). Integrating models of diffusion of innovations: A conceptual framework. *Annual Review of Sociology, 28*, 297–326.

Wittgenstein, L. (1958). *The blue and brown books*. New York: Harper Collins Publishers.

Xing, J., Wang, W., Zhao, W., Huang, J. (2009). A novel multi-touch human-computer-interface based on binocular stereo vision. *IEEE International Intelligence Ubiquitous Computing and Education*, 319–323.

Chapter 3
New Technologies in British Pharmacy Practice

Kimberly Jamie

Abstract Despite its centrality to the patient illness trajectory, pharmacy is a fairly neglected area of research in the social sciences. Yet, community and hospital pharmacy are sectors in which innovative practices and technological artefacts regularly reshape and reorganise everyday work and relationships. Drawing on semi-structured interviews with 38 practitioners from a variety of medical and scientific backgrounds, this chapter explores the ways in which various new pharmacy technologies are defined by both bureaucratic medicines management/pharmaceutical care policy and everyday working practices. It argues that pharmacy practice has been extensively reorganised around an increased clinical focus, in which new technologies have played a central role through two epistemic groups of innovations- technologies of clinical practice, and technologies enabling clinical practice. The 'reflexive monitoring' and 'contextual integration' constructs of May and Finch's normalisation process theory (NPT) are used here as a framework for understanding the evaluative work which is carried out in everyday community and hospital pharmacy practice.

Keywords Pharmacy • Hospital • Community • Medicines management • Pharmaceutical care

3.1 Introduction: Pharmacy Practice in Britain

Over the past 30 years, British pharmacy, particularly in the community setting has undergone major changes with regards to the everyday management of medications and patient health. The modern incarnation of community pharmacy can be traced to the mid-1980s when uncertainty about the future of community pharmacy practice was addressed through the UK National Pharmacy Association's

K. Jamie (✉)
University of York, York, UK
e-mail: kimberly.jamie@york.ac.uk

K. Wasen (ed.), *Emerging Health Technology*, SpringerBriefs in Health Care Management and Economics, DOI: 10.1007/978-3-642-32570-0_3, © The Author(s) 2013

1982 Ask Your Pharmacist campaign. This initiative encouraged the public to utilise their local pharmacy and was followed in the 1990s by the implementation of the 'extended role'. This extended role was grounded in what has become widely known in pharmacy practice research as the Nuffield Report (1986) and later expounded in other policy publications (Department of Health and Royal Pharmaceutical Society of Great Britain 1992; Royal Pharmaceutical Society of Great Britain 1995). The implementation of the suggestions from these reports culminated with community pharmacists' role being expanded to include increased clinical work through prescribed medicines management; chronic illness management; common ailments management and the promotion of healthy lifestyles (Harding and Taylor 1997). This extended role, and the initiatives which existed around it, reconfigured community pharmacists as healthcare practitioners and relocated them outside of the dispensary, thus discursively positing them as a 'first port of call' for patients (Anderson 2001: 23).

In hospital settings, the 1970s were crucial to the development of contemporary pharmacy practice. During the period in between the establishment of the UK National Health Service (NHS) in 1948 and the publication of the Noel Hall Report in 1970, hospital pharmacy was organised at the local level of the individual hospital. As such, there was a relative lack of standardisation in the profession and concerns around poor job prospects and low pay overshadowed attempts, such as agreeing national pay scales, to standardised and expand the sector (Anderson 2001). In response to concerns about hospital pharmacy, the Noel Hall Report (Hall 1970) recommended that hospital pharmacy should be organised at the regional level under the management of an Area Pharmaceutical Officer with every 4,000–6,000 hospital beds being served by around eight pharmacists. Additionally, it was suggested that new salary structures for principle pharmacists, staff pharmacists and pharmacy technicians and on-going training reviews would make hospital pharmacy a more appealing career for young people (Levitt 1976; Stone and Curtis 2002). At the end of the 1970s, most hospital pharmacists were routinely practising ward pharmacy (i.e. dispensing medications and offering medications counselling on wards rather than in the dispensary), which later discursively evolved into clinical pharmacy and during the following decades the profession became increasingly characterised by clinical specialisation in fields such as oncology or paediatrics (Anderson 2001).

Although British community and hospital pharmacists share a common undergraduate education programme, the everyday work of community and hospital pharmacists in the UK is highly divergent. Bhakta (2010) specifically highlights working patterns, patients and medicines as three key areas where community and hospital pharmacy practice diverge. As such, whilst community pharmacists tend to work in relative isolation (also see Cooper et al. 2009) and focus on chronic conditions and medications, those practising in hospital settings work in a more inter-disciplinary environment which is typified by acutely ill patients and their more complex medication regimes. Moreover, the technologies which are central to the everyday work of pharmacists are also different in community and hospital settings and this chapter argues that this divergence can be understood in line with the formal policies which underpin practice in these different settings.

Pharmacists interact with various technologies in their everyday practice as part of their focus on medications and their associated 'stuff' (Barber 2005). In the community setting, the extended role of British pharmacists has necessitated their increased use of a variety of diagnostic devices such as carbon monoxide monitors, blood glucose tests and pregnancy testing kits. In hospitals, technologies which have impacted on pharmacy practice have, for the most part, tended to be less clinical and more operational. As such, innovative technologies in hospital pharmacy practice have tended to be centred on dispensing practices rather than testing and monitoring devices. Dispensing robots, electronic prescribing systems and computerised medical records are clear examples of this.

Innovative technologies in pharmacy can act to reconfigure the occupational role and identity of the profession. This process of defining professional boundaries and jurisdictions of various practices through innovations has been explored elsewhere (Korica and Molloy 2010; Mclaughlin and Webster 1998; Zetka 2001) but the implementation and effects of technology in pharmacy have not been extensively analysed. Most of the research that does exist in this area tends to focus on the macro-level of the pharmacy sector in its entirety rather than the micro-level work which is carried out to integrate technologies, and their effects, into practice. This reflects a wider paucity of attention given to how technology features in the routine practice of medical professionals, through which Heath et al. (2003:1881) argue technology 'gains its significance'.

In an attempt to fill this paucity of research, this chapter examines the ways in which new technologies are configured into everyday pharmacy working practice in community and hospital settings. May and Finch's (2009) normalisation process theory (NPT) provides useful insights for conceptualising the ways in which new technologies are integrated into everyday pharmacy work as some of the components (constructs) of NPT resonate with much of the empirical data collected here. In particular, the notions of 'coherence', 'reflexive monitoring' and 'contextual integration' are mobilised to analyse the ways in which new technologies are defined and evaluated by pharmacy practitioners.

The chapter is informed by qualitative interview data obtained from 38 semi-structured interviews with diverse practitioners (10 pharmacogeneticists; 2 oncologists; 2 general medical practitioners (GPs); 4 pharmacy stakeholders; 10 community pharmacists and 10 hospital pharmacists) and examines the ways in which diverse technologies have reshaped the everyday work of pharmacists working in community and hospital settings in the UK.

3.2 Defining New Technologies in Pharmacy: Discourses of Medicines Management and Pharmaceutical Care

The process of defining new technologies in pharmacy is central to their configuration as useful or otherwise for everyday working practices. May and Finch (2009) conceptualise this process of defining new technologies or interventions as 'coherence' work where work is undertaken to define and organise the meaning, uses and utility of a practice through which it is made possible. As an example, in a study of stepped-care for depression Franx et al. (2012) mobilise the coherence construct of NPT to examine the ways in which depression is conceptualised by healthcare professionals. This process of defining depression creates shared definitions of, and boundaries between, patients who are depressed and patients who are not as well as shared measures of the severity of depression.

In the case of new technologies in pharmacy practice, coherence work is linked with the sector into which these new technologies are being implemented. In other words, the distinction between community and hospital pharmacy becomes apparent through the different ways in which new innovations are defined in these settings. This divergent coherence work is related to the divergent nature of practice, medicines and patients in these settings as highlighted by Bhakta (2010). Here, the discourses of pharmaceutical care and medicines management become important in the process of defining innovations. Although these two notions are subject to multiple definitions and are often used inter-changeably Barber (2001) argues that the rhetoric of pharmaceutical care is focused on individualised patient-centric medicines efficacy and risk, whilst that of medicines management is related to organisational interests in improved medicines efficacy. Hence, the discourses of pharmaceutical care can be understood to underpin community pharmacy practice whilst medicines management is more discursively aligned with hospital pharmacy.

3.2.1 Defining New Technologies in Hospital Pharmacy: Medicines Management

Within this, medicines management in hospital pharmacy is grounded in organisational interests in medicines efficacy, where therapy decisions are based around local policies and financial implications. Moreover, risk management in this practice model is located within legal and corporate responsibilities, as Hospital Pharmacist 1 (a chief pharmacist suggests):

> You have corporate responsibility for medicines management in the Trust...If something goes wrong with medicines within the Trust it's the Chief Executive and myself who are ultimately responsible. We are the ones who end up in court and ultimately in prison (HP1).

In this vein, the implementation of innovative practice technologies in hospital pharmacy is understood as a way of both streamlining dispensing practices in order to improve overall pharmacy efficiency and improving and monitoring dispensing quality, as Hospital Pharmacist 6 says,

> The computer does all that [inputs prescription details such as dates and signatures] for you which means that we've been able to focus the pharmacist resource more on safety and appropriateness of drug treatment. HP6

And the way the information can be used in terms of we can do audits that were impossible to do previously HP6.

Here, the electronic patient record and the computer system on which it depends are defined through formalised policy rhetoric as technological instruments which can make more efficient use of staff resources and assist with better quality audit activities. On a less formalised level of everyday practice, these technologies are central to generating individualised discourses of toxicity for patient bodies where this toxicity is managed through the application and mobilisation of these technologies, as Hospital Pharmacist 6 highlights in reference to electronic prescribing systems:

Under electronic prescriptions and administration records... And that's made a massive difference in terms of the information you can present to prescribers at the point their doing prescriptions about interactions and allergies and all sorts of other things HP6

Another example of this is computerised labelling. Labelling work has always been a central feature of pharmacy practice and it is, in part, through such labelling practices that pharmacists enact a key part of their professional identity—the symbolic transformation of chemicals into culturally meaningful objects of drugs (Dingwall and Wilson 1995). Labelling work, then, locates medications within patients' wider 'lifeworlds' where, through dosage and administration details, medicines become social objects to be integrated into everyday 'dimensions' of patients' lives (see Cribb 2011: 38). The implementation of computerised labelling represents a paradigmatic shift in labelling practice and is operationalised in line with formalised medicines management policies where computer-generated (rather than hand-written) labels are thought be clearer, thus making medicines easier for patients to engage with and adhere to (Shrank et al. 2007a). In this way, computerised labelling is grounded in an organisational focus on reducing the cost and time burden of patients inadvertently under- or over-dosing due to disengagement with medications regimen. Moreover, Shrank et al. (2007b) note that effective labelling is central to toxicity management as, in contrast to Patient Information Leaflets, medication labels are part of the medication object itself given that labels cannot as easily be separated from medications. The comment from Hospital Pharmacist 4 highlights the impact of electronic medication labelling;

When I started we had typewriters. From that point of view technology has really improved in terms of...patient labelling HP4

3.2.2 Innovative Drug Technologies in Hospital Pharmacy

This focus on computerised labelling attests to the fact that much of the emphasis on new technologies in pharmacy is centred around non-medicinal devices and black-boxed artefacts. Medications and their potential toxicities are, however, the primary specialist area of pharmacists and are the means through which the patient body comes into being in everyday pharmacy practice.

Given this, much of the data collected from hospital pharmacists is concerned with new drug technologies, which is to say new pharmaceutical products that reorganise or reconfigure pharmacy work. Within this, the discourse of toxicity around these new drug technologies is central to their reorganisational capacity. As such, these new drugs represent new ways of constructing and managing toxicity. The most pertinent example of this to be highlighted is monoclonal antibody (mAb) technology. This field of drug technology specifically targets areas of single proteins (epitopes) which are over-expressed as a result of disease. Hence, monoclonal antibody drugs do not rely on the 'shotgun' approach of, for example, cytotoxic medications and, as a result, are less likely to cause adverse effects (Keller 2009).

Given this, mAbs are operationalised within formal medicines management policy as a way to reduce the financial burden of adverse drug effects and to improve the patient experience of their medications regime. They are also important because they are seen to enable more targeted, individualised treatment regimes. This is reflected in the way that mAbs are most commonly prescribed to cancer patients whose bodies are understood by multiple medical gazes as particularly complex and risk-laden in terms of their morbidity, but made more so given the effects of traditional chemotherapy regimes. Pharmacogeneticist 10 (who has a particular interest in oncology) highlights this;

> We give them enough drugs to just not quite kill them but actually sometimes it's the drugs that kill you and not the cancer so we need to try and get away from that because there's more morbidity associated with the drugs PGx10

Hence, the prescription of mAbs is understood as a positive step in cancer care given their reduced toxicity, as Hospital Pharmacist 8 highlights;

> I know that you've got your monoclonal antibodies now and they are not without their side effects but they are in many ways superior in terms of side effect profiles to conventional chemotherapy HP8

This perceived superiority to traditional cytotoxic medications is discursively aligned with increasingly targeted prescription behaviour patterns where a 'molecular gaze' is adopted by prescribers in making therapy decisions. Rose (2007) argues that this molecular gaze sits within a more general molecular 'style of thought' (see Fleck 1979) that underpins contemporary medical practice. Given this 'style of thought' in treatment decisions, what we might call 'the pharmacy gaze' has also become increasingly molecularised with the pharmacological action of drugs, and their potential toxicities, being understood at the molecular level. Hence, the discourse of toxicity around mAbs is created based on the molecular characteristics of the patient body, which are identified through testing for specific biomarkers, as in the case of pre-prescription HER2 testing for Herceptin regimes. Hospital Pharmacist 9 (an oncology pharmacist) demonstrates this well;

> MAbs where you are focusing on markers and testing. For the conventional chemo type drugs there's no way of predicting which patients are going to do well with this treatment and so you end up giving it to everybody HP9

This quote also highlights the paradigmatic shift in oncology practice from "willy-nilly" (HP9) universal chemotherapy regimens to increasingly molecularised and individualised courses of therapy. While, at first site, more individualised treatment regimes might be presumed to be expensive, from the perspective of formalised medicines management, such an approach reduces cost because of the reduction of adverse drug effects:

> So it's all now about targeted therapies…And it's good because it means that you don't over treat patients. You're not treating patients willy-nilly. I think it's good because it's a lot more individualised now in terms of making sure that patients get the treatments that are best for them HP9

Given this decreased propensity for toxicity, mAbs can potentially reconfigure the everyday work of pharmacy by refocusing work away from the management of adverse drug effects which has previously been central to oncology pharmacy practice. Moreover, this decreased toxicity and the potential for mAbs to be administered to patients orally means that there is a drive towards relocating oncology medication administration away from the hospital (So 2010). In moving towards the administration of relatively low toxicity medications outside of the hospital setting, these drugs are made meaningful to patients through their existence within their wider 'lifeworld'. So (2010: 35) also highlights the way in which this relocation of medications is defined through formal medicines management policies and organisational interests as a 'more cost effective way' of treating oncology patients.

3.2.3 Defining New Technologies in Community Pharmacy: Pharmaceutical Care

The implementation of technologies into community pharmacy ought to be treated as a separate phenomenon given the difference in practice between community and hospital practice. The introduction of new technologies in community practice is, then, centred around two primary concerns; the pharmaceutical care of individual patients vis-à-vis potential drug reactions, and the increase in clinical practice, the latter of which is explored in more detail below.

The discourses and practices of pharmaceutical care are central to the process of defining new technologies in community pharmacy. Similar to the medicines management rhetoric mobilised in hospital pharmacy, pharmaceutical care processes are central to the operationalisation of new technologies in everyday community practice. The data suggest that the most pertinent example of this is the implementation of computer systems where the community pharmacy computer is understood as a means to improve pharmaceutical care, patient adherence and outcomes and reduce toxicity through various functions and packages.

The arrival of computer systems in community pharmacy represents a significant departure from traditional experiences of pharmacy work, in which manual documentation and procedures played a central role and underpinned much of the

GP/pharmacist communication (see Motulsky et al. 2008). Writing some years ago, Foster (1992) noted that producing labels, storing patient prescription information, producing patient safety documentation and managing stock were the key areas that applications of computer technology addressed in pharmacy; the data collected here suggest that these work activities are still the primary applications of computer technology in community pharmacy.

Making sense of the meaning and significance of computerisation of community pharmacy is strongly linked with pharmaceutical care processes and discourses through the use of computers to identify potential drug toxicity. Within this, the pharmacy computer is framed as advantageous in its capacity to store patient medication records and algorithmic information which can help identify potential drug interactions. In doing so, the community pharmacy computer is understood as a way to improve pharmaceutical care by increasing patient and practitioner awareness of potential toxicity (Abarca et al. 2006). This is in addition to the capacity for electronically producing labels and safety information, which is central to patient adherence and outcomes policies.

In everyday practice, the community pharmacy computer is operationalised as a documentary space for the recording and management of toxicity which at the same time brings the patient body to life through its presence within this toxicity documentary. The community pharmacy computer, then, is used to store patient drug histories which construct a discourse of toxicity through the identification of potentially harmful drug interactions. Within the documentary space of this drug history the patient body is configured as a complex site of potential toxicity to be managed by the community pharmacist through labelling, advice and counselling. Community Pharmacist 2 highlights the centrality of the computer to toxicity management in contemporary community pharmacy practice;

> I think the computer coming into the pharmacy opened so many doors really. Prior to that we didn't even have a record of what patients had ever had. We'd nothing to help us with drug interactions. We'd no computer to flash up warnings. I mean, I often think—well I worry, to be honest—how much harm we did to patients because of drug interactions that we never even—we may have known about but not to the extent that we do today. And we had nothing to remind us of them at all. We didn't put particular patient warnings on labels CP2.

Defining the utility and meaning of new technologies in pharmacy is a process which sits within both formalised pharmaceutical care and medicines management practices and more informal, individualised everyday work practices. Within formalised medicines management and pharmaceutical care rhetoric and practices, the integration of new technologies into pharmacy is operationalised as a way to improve the safety and efficacy of pharmacy dispensing. At a less formalised level of everyday practice, new technologies act as inscription devices to configure the patient body as a set of particular risks and toxicities which are managed through discourses of toxicity. Moreover, in community pharmacy new technologies can also act to reshape pharmacy practice towards a more clinical focus. It is to this application of technology that the chapter now turns.

3.3 Technologies and Clinical Practice

Changes that have occurred, and continue to occur, in everyday pharmacy work are multi-dimensional and arise from both macro and micro policies and strategies such as the Department of Health and Royal Pharmaceutical Society of Great Britain's (as was) extended role. One key way in which pharmacy work and relations have been reorganised in the last three decades is in its more clinical focus, in which new technologies have played a central role.

New technologies are central to this more clinical reorganisation of pharmacy in two key ways and, once again, emphasise the distinction between community and hospital pharmacy practice. In one way, new technologies which are central to clinical activities have become increasingly present in (particularly community) pharmacy; these are conceptualised here technologies of clinical work. In another way, technologies such as electronic prescribing and pharmacy robots are conceptualised as central actors in the process of reorganising (particularly hospital) pharmacy work. As such, new innovations are understood as reorganising pharmacy work towards an increased clinical focus by removing pharmacists from the dispensary and what Hospital Pharmacist Six describes as "traffic warden duties" and increasing their clinical workload; these are understood here as technologies enabling clinical work. Each of these is taken in turn.

3.3.1 Technologies of Clinical Work: Configuring the Individual and Public Health Body in the Community Pharmacy

New technologies are central to much of the clinical work that pharmacists, particularly in the community setting, now undertake as part of their everyday practice. These black-boxed devices, such as blood glucose and carbon monoxide monitors, act as new ways of knowing the patient body. Moreover, given their association with the maintenance of health and wellbeing, they also act to reconfigure the pharmacist as a health promotion or public health practitioner. Through this reconfiguration, pharmacy practice becomes less spatially-bound to the dispensary and is increasingly practised in the consultation room (in the case of community pharmacy) and at the patient bedside (in the case of hospital pharmacy).

The clinical role of community pharmacists has created new ways through which pharmacists interact with, and come to know, patient bodies. The outputs from black-boxed clinical devices, such as those mentioned above, provide patients and pharmacists with access to biomedical knowledge about patient bodies. Unlike in hospital pharmacy and GP work, this knowledge does not necessarily feed into prescription decisions but instead becomes central to the individual patient health project and risk profile. In this way, the clinical monitoring work that is undertaken by community pharmacists can be understood as sitting within a health promotion and surveillance medicine approach where the 'extracorporal space', otherwise referred to as 'lifestyle' (Armstrong 1995: 401), becomes important in the pharmacists' configuration of, and interaction with, the patient body. Through testing and monitoring individual patient bodies, what we can call a collective public health body is created which is located within wider public health discourses and foci.

This public health work represents a significant shift in the focus of pharmacy practice beyond the medication needs of patients, which is highly spatially-bound to the dispensary, to one that incorporates the wider 'lifeworld' of patients and the impact this has on health. Such an example of this is provided by Community Pharmacist 2 who ran a health promotion clinic which mobilised a number of devices to provide patients with knowledge about their own bodies, which was then used for health advice. In this monitoring clinic, blood pressure, blood glucose and cholesterol monitoring kits and scales were used to configure the patient as a set of health risks and behaviours which could be managed by the pharmacist;

> Just come along, get your blood pressure taken, get your blood glucose/cholesterol done and we'll give you a bit of healthy lifestyle advice, etc.... We did it for about eight or nine months and it was really popular. We got husbands and wives coming together in the evening, which was great. Because we used to say, well, your cholesterol may be up, do you eat a lot of cheese? The husband would say no and the wife would say yes you do... this is something new for pharmacy CP2

This quote demonstrates that monitoring devices and the 'extracorporeal space' (in this case regarding eating habits) are central to clinical community pharmacy work and the public health body it constructs. Moreover, Community Pharmacist 2's reflection suggests a significant practice shift from the traditional role of pharmacists to this more public health or health promotion oriented focus, through which individual patient's health profiles and the collective public health body are brought into being. Elsewhere, the relationship between public health and medical practice more generally (Armstrong 1995) and public health and pharmacy (Anderson 2007) have been explored. In the case of public health and pharmacy research, however, there is a marked absence of the patient body through which public health discourses are enacted in the pharmacy setting. Just as an analysis of medicines management is limited without the presence of a medications using patient body, neither can public health practice be fully analysed without a body, or collective of bodies, discursively constructed by public health concerns.

Whereas the focus of traditional pharmacy practice centres on individual patient bodies as sites of medications use and potential toxicity, the public health and health promotion focus of practice is centred on multiple bodies and their collective relationship with wider public health foci. As such, the testing and monitoring technologies that are central to the performance of clinical pharmacy activities configure both individual health and risk profiles and a collective public health and risk profile which feeds into macro and meso level public health strategies. The following quote from Community Pharmacist 2 demonstrates the way in which the individual health profile and the collective public health body are created through testing and monitoring activities;

so they [patients] just used to go away with their own results. We kept a copy of the results because we had to give that anonymised information to the PCT CP2.

This type of clinical work in community pharmacy has previously fed into questions around boundary encroachment (Eaton and Webb 1979; Edmunds and Calnan 2001) and the General Pharmaceutical Council recently argued that pharmacists are not competent to 'undertake a physical examination which includes the touching of a patient's body' (General Pharmaceutical Council 2012: 122). These concerns are located within a relatively rigid model of primary care practice in which GPs' relative power is seen as at risk from disadvantageous jurisdictional realignments. Contrary to this, however, Community Pharmacist 2 notes that pharmacists' relative professional status (which is, generally speaking, lower than that of GPs) can be advantageous for engaging patients in public health and health promotion activities, in which technological devices play a key role:

And people do sometimes feel less worried about coming into that kind of environment than going to the GP practice... Pharmacy can actually play a part in health promotion like that if people are more willing to come and see it as less official than going to the doctors' practices I think CP2

This notion was also suggested by Community Pharmacist 1 who notes that pharmacists utilising flu vaccination technologies enabled a wider population to have the vaccine than would have done if this remained a GP activity. Through administering vaccinations, the activities of pharmacists are placed within the boundaries of public health practices and their role in configuring, and managing the public health body is fore grounded. This also supports Taylor's (2005: 292) vision of the community pharmacist as 'the people's doctor' and, elsewhere, the benefits of pharmacists' involvement with vaccination programmes and technologies have been noted (Steyer et al. 2004);

Some of the larger Boots [a large UK chain of pharmacies] stores have got involved in administering flu vaccines...the flu vaccinations enabled a few more people to get vaccinated who wouldn't otherwise have been able to CP1

Clinical devices are, then, central to the construction of the public health body in community pharmacy. Within this, potential toxicity is understood as a risk not just of medications and the body's relationship to them but through the body's characteristics which are defined within public health and health promotion norms and discourses. These characteristics, such as weight, body mass index and cholesterol levels, are then made socially meaningful as characteristics of a public health body through these clinical devices. In other words, the public health body comes into being through the outputs from clinical devices and the relationship of these outputs with wider public health foci. Whereas the complexity of the body in pharmacy is traditionally rooted in potential drug interactions arising from the body as a site of medications use, clinical community pharmacy operationalises the complexity of the public health body as being rooted in these characteristics and the health risks that it presents.

In this sense, the focus of clinical community pharmacy is strongly linked with the traditional focus of community pharmacy in that it is, at the base level, concerned with toxicity. The departure, then, comes from the relationship with the patient body which is enacted through the technologies of clinical work. These technologies broaden the definition of risk in community pharmacy to being linked with patient lifestyles and 'extracorporeal spaces' rather than just medications and their interactions. May and Finch (2009) note that a central part of coherence work is defining innovations by their differences from existing practices. In this case, the reconfiguration of pharmacy work to focus on the public health body is defined by its difference from traditional pharmacy work which focuses on medications and their toxicities alone. This reshaping of pharmacy's focus is aligned with macro-level policies, such as the provision of essential services through the extended role, and micro-level work activities, such as providing specialist clinics.

3.3.2 Technologies Enabling Clinical Work: Practising Away from the Dispensary

The second category of clinical technologies in pharmacy is what can be conceptualised as technologies enabling clinical work. One of the most significant shifts in both hospital and community pharmacy work is the relocation of pharmacy practice, and practitioners, away from the dispensary. Increasingly pharmacy practice takes place in more clinical locations, namely the consultation room in the case of community pharmacy and at the bedside in the case of hospital pharmacy. Increased patient contact at these locations is understood as an effective method for managing drug toxicity as risks are increasingly communicated to patients by active face-to-face counselling by the pharmacist rather than through passive patient information leaflets. This method of managing toxicity is thought to encourage concordance, improve patients' experiences of their illness and medicines and reduce the financial burden of drug-related readmissions (for example Bajramovic et al. 2004). This sense of the effectiveness of face-to-face clinical work and counselling is encapsulated by Hospital Pharmacist 1 (a chief pharmacist);

> It's all about asset stripping staff out of the dispensary and getting them to be able to work on the ward...you cannot do effective medicines management in the dispensary (HP1)

This relocation of pharmacists away from the dispensary is primarily facilitated through the integration of new technologies, such as dispensing robots and electronic prescribing and labelling services, which perform a number of the functions previously undertaken by dispensary-bound pharmacists.

Such technologies are more commonly associated with hospital pharmacy and sit within the formal medicines management policies of hospital Trusts. The integration of these technologies reconfigures the role and position of pharmacists within the hospital practice structure given their fairly high integration in hospital healthcare teams (see for example Makowsky et al. 2009). Given this, the use of such technologies in pharmacy can be understood in line with the collective action aspect of NPT (May and Finch 2009). According to May and Finch (2009: 544) when new technologies are integrated into everyday practices, work is undertaken to 'reorganize relationships' which 'involves collective purposive action aimed at some goal'. In this case, the goal is the increased pharmacy clinical work and patient contact where relationships are reorganised around the integration of pharmacists within the hospital healthcare team. As such, the relational integration of these new technologies is mediated by an understanding of their being necessary for improved medicines management within hospital clinical pharmacy.

Hospital Pharmacist 1 demonstrates the way in which local relationships (between pharmacists and other healthcare practitioners and between pharmacists and patients) are reconfigured by the presence of technologies enabling clinical work and the subsequent movement of pharmacists out of the dispensary:

> So we're investing quite heavily in technology. We've got very sensible computer systems to support the dispensing processes. We'll be getting a robot in the next few months to make sure that that's all automated. It's all about asset stripping staff out of the dispensary and getting them to be able to work on the wards HP1

The integration of these technologies has also altered the sorts of everyday activities that hospital pharmacists undertake. Hospital Pharmacist 6 notes that the entrance of the computer into hospital pharmacy has shifted the focus of pharmacists' work away from somewhat mundane activities which can now be effectively enacted by technological devices. Hospital Pharmacist 6 locates these activities within the pharmacists' 'checking' role as "traffic warden duties" and defines the use of a computer for them as beneficial for medicines management and safety processes:

> It's what I describe as prescribing traffic warden duties, if you like. It's everything written in block capitals, can you read it, has the doctor signed it, has it got a date on it, are the doctor's intentions clear?...the computer does all that for you which means that we've been able to focus the pharmacist resource more on safety and appropriateness of drug treatment rather than dotting i's and crossing t's and writing the print names in block capitals like we used to do. HP6

In this quote, the clinical work of pharmacists is privileged over dispensary-bound checking duties where the former is understood as a more effective use of pharmacy resources. These sentiments are echoed by Hospital Pharmacist 4 vis-a-vis dispensing robots;

> From the point of view of [the] department probably yes. Releasing staff to other duties I think it's probably going to be beneficial HP4

Pharmacy robots have received some attention in the academic literature. In their study of hospital pharmacy robots in two UK hospital pharmacies, Barrett et al. (2011) note that pharmacy robots reorganise professional relationships throughout the hospital structure. In this way, pharmacists became further integrated into medical teams and increased their 'institutional legitimacy within the hospital' (p. 13) whilst pharmacy assistants expanded their jurisdiction into knowledge of robotics. Hence, the collective action involved in integrating pharmacy robots into everyday work is far-reaching yet ubiquitously underpinned by the need to reduce prescribing errors and improve medicines management as per local and national policies (see Audit Commission 2001).

3.3.3 Analysing Robot Technologies in Pharmacy?

The implementation of dispensing robots, and other clinical technologies, in routine pharmacy practice could be analysed from an actor-network theory (ANT) perspective. Briefly, ANT is premised on the notion that the social world and social relations within it are constituted by networks of heterogeneous actants. These actants can be either human or nonhuman since it is the capacity for enabling action which is central to the actant's existence within the network. Hence, reflexivity and intentionality are not essential characteristics of actants, which means that anything can be an actant provided it 'is granted to be the source of action' (Latour, cited in Cerulo 2009: 534). In an analysis of metered dosage inhalers (MDIs), Prout (1996: 210) notes that the MDI network is constituted by a complex set of associations between a large number of human and nonhuman actants which are 'mutually configured in the process'. As such, the MDI network is constituted by designers, clinicians, patients, patients' families, nurses, pharmacists, MDIs, monitoring devices and instructional documentation, the qualities of all of which are configured through, and within, this network. There is a compelling argument for understanding pharmacy robots, and other clinical technologies, from an ANT perspective as actants with the hospital network given their centrality to everyday pharmacy work and processes.

However, constructivist perspectives, such as ANT, have been subject to critique for their understanding of artefacts as nothing more than a sum of the interpretations and negotiations which happen around them. Hutchby (2003) draws on the field of the psychology of perceptions to offer a middle ground theory between realism and constructivism in the understanding of technologies. In a direct critique of Grint and Woolgar's (1997) 'technologies as text' perspective (i.e. where technologies ought to be understood as texts written by producers and read by consumers), he argues that the constructivist understanding of technologies as tabulae rasa is limited in its failure to acknowledge that technologies posses properties outside of interpretations of them. As Rappert (2003: 566), in his response to Hutchby points out, 'interpretations of technology are still interpretations of something and what that 'something' is must be acknowledged'. In not proposing a return to determinist understanding of technology, Hutchby suggests that technologies possess different 'affordances' (that is to say possibilities for action) which frame, but do not determine, action related to them.

Hutchby's middle ground perspective offers a more useful way to approach an analysis of technologies in pharmacy as the data resonate with the idea that technologies offer different affordances to different actors in different contexts. As such, when technologies are located within formalised medicines management arenas by those with increased, and corporate, medicines management responsibilities (i.e. chief pharmacists and hospital chief executives), they afford the possibility of improving organisational medicines management processes and efficiency throughout the pharmacy department. In another arena, the location of technologies in everyday practice of pharmacy affords the possibility of shifting the location, and nature, of everyday pharmacy work away from dispensary-based activities to more clinical patient engagement. In this way, a technology such as a pharmacy robot may be seen by different actors as affording different actions; whilst the chief pharmacist might see the possibility of reducing drug-related morbidity statistics; the pharmacists might see the possibility of an increased clinical workload; and the pharmacy technician might see the possibility of becoming a skilled robotics engineer.

So far, this chapter has demonstrated that innovations in pharmacy are key elements in changing pharmacy practice and are central to the reorganisation of pharmacy work and relations around a more clinical focus. This clinical reorganisation is centred on two epistemic groups of technologies- those of clinical practice and those enabling clinical practice away from the dispensary. The discursive construction of technological innovation in pharmacy tends to be centred around a focus on reducing toxicity and improving patient experience, with regards to both medications and health and lifestyle more generally (through the collective public health body). In this way, the rationale behind innovation in pharmacy is informed by formalised pharmaceutical care and medicines management policies and these also construct a framework through with innovations are evaluated and appraised by pharmacy practitioners. Here, again, NPT provides a useful framework for analysing this evaluative work through its 'reflexive monitoring' and 'contextual integration' constructs.

3.4 Reflexive Monitoring and the Integration of New Technologies in Pharmacy

May and Finch (2009) argue that 'reflexive monitoring' is the process through which technological innovations are both formally and informally evaluated. Within this, judgements are made as to the effectiveness and utility of a new practice, based on 'socially patterned and institutionally shared beliefs' (May and Finch 2009: 545). Related to this, 'contextual integration' refers to the incorporation of a practice within a particular social context. They argue that innovations can impact upon existing structures and procedures in a given work context and affect the mechanisms of material and symbolic resourcing. Here, they use the example of the implementation of teledermatology services (the replacement of in-person skin disease diagnosis with remote diagnosis using digital images (see Finch 2008)) to show that innovations which add complexity and workload to existing practices may fail to be fully integrated into a given work context. These notions of 'reflexive monitoring' and 'contextual integration' offer a useful framework for understanding why some technologies are integrated into everyday pharmacy practice (or 'normalised') and others are not.

According to May and Finch, reflexive monitoring is undertaken through both communal and individual appraisal techniques, which can be understood as mapping onto formalised bureaucratic medicines management processes and professional discursive practices of everyday work. Hence, communal appraisal involves assessment within an organisational context and mobilises formalised 'mechanisms of institutional knowledge production' whilst individual appraisal involves discursive judgements about the value and outcomes of an innovation which are rooted in individual practices (May and Finch 2009: 546). Here, then the communal appraisal process can be understood as sitting within formal, organisational medicines management policy whilst individual appraisal can be related to informal processes of everyday practice enacted through innovative technologies.

The present data demonstrate that pharmacists undertake reflexive monitoring through both communal and individual appraisal in their everyday interactions with new technologies. As a result of this reflexive monitoring process, some innovations fail to be normalised in everyday practice. Two examples of this were highlighted by Community Pharmacist 1 in discussing the drugs Zocor (to treat cholesterol and coronary heart disease) and Clamelle (to treat Chlamydia). In both of these instances, pre-prescription testing is undertaken to determine the appropriateness of the drug. In the case of Zocor, which was declassified to an over-the-counter medication in 2004, this is done by the pharmacist constructing a patient risk profile through a pre-prescription consultation. In the case of Clamelle, this is testing done by the patient following the purchase of a testing kit from the pharmacy. In cases where the patient tests positive for Chlamydia, they can then return to the pharmacy to purchase the necessary antibiotics. In both of these cases, Community Pharmacist 1 notes that these "didn't really take off" and "didn't make a massive impact".

This lack of normalisation can be understood as related to the professional jurisdictions that are relatively rigidly enacted in the community setting. In this division of labour, pre-prescription testing is a work activity most commonly associated with GPs and located within particular healthcare settings. The reallocation of testing activities to pharmacists and patients for these particular innovations can be understood as a potential barrier to their normalisation;

> It [Zocor] was something they could get with less hassle from the doctors and the doctor was able to arrange the necessary blood tests to do this CP1

This quote highlights the inconvenience and limited capacity of pharmacy testing as features for Zocor's lack of normalisation. This can be analysed within May and Finch's (2009: 545) notion of 'contextual integration' whereby innovations are incorporated into a social context where new work is linked with existing structures and procedures. In this case, the declassification of Zocor did not incorporate pre-prescription blood testing into pharmacy practice. Given this, Community Pharmacist 1 highlights the comparative ease with which Zocor, and similar medicines, can be accessed in contexts where pre-prescription testing is already an integrated practice in everyday work, namely through GPs.

Moreover, these examples demonstrate the issues that can occur when work activities necessitated by an innovation (in this case pre-prescription testing) are outside of a traditional professional jurisdiction. As such, the location of pre-prescription testing work within the professional boundaries of general medical practice suggests that the requirement for pre-prescription consultations in the community pharmacy and Clamelle's requirement for patients to self-test at home represent too much of a divergence from the community division of labour in which pre-prescription testing is carried out by the GP. Community Pharmacist 10 also highlights this issue of innovations representing a practice outside of the traditional division of labour;

> You have to question whether patients would come to the pharmacy to get a test done when they could get it done at the doctors CP10

Reflexive monitoring in hospital pharmacy highlights the individual appraisal process which is carried out in conjunction with more communal evaluations of the value of new innovations. In their study of hospital pharmacy robots, Barrett et al. (2011) juxtapose the communal appraisal of robotic innovations, which are grounded in government priorities for reducing dispensing errors and improving pharmacy efficiency, with individual appraisals grounded in the routine work of dispensing, loading the robot and dealing with malfunctions. Here, then, the interplay of communal and individual appraisal processes can be seen. The data here present a similar story. As such, innovations are communally appraised through the rhetoric of formalised policies as beneficial for medicines management, staff resourcing and pharmacy efficiency, as the above quote from Hospital Pharmacist 1 highlights.

Running concurrently to this communal appraisal is a more individual process of evaluation where innovations are judged against wider expectations of the professional practice of pharmacy and the management of everyday work activities.

As described above, the implementation of technology into pharmacy practice is central to the increased clinical role of the sector. It is also through defining this increased clinical work as a central feature of contemporary pharmacy practice that appraisals of the value of new innovations are enabled. In other words, as the boundaries of pharmacy practice shift to incorporate increased clinical work the value of new innovations is measured against expectations about what pharmacy is, or should be given this restructured division of labour. As an example, Community Pharmacist 2 discusses computer technology as an aid to clinical work and states that "It's basically unrecognisable from how pharmacy used to be, which is brilliant" (CP2). Within this appraisal, the implementation of computer technology is understood to have had a key role in shifting the boundaries of what constitutes pharmacy practice. This strategy in pharmacy is described by Birenbaum (1990) as a 'collective mobility project'.

In other instances, however, this collective mobility towards clinical practice, facilitated by technological innovations, can have a more negative register and be associated with deskilling. As such, technology in pharmacy is evaluated as artefacts through, and within, which ideas about what pharmacy practices is, and should be, are positioned too far from pharmacy's core focus on medications and their 'stuff' (see Barber 2005). Hospital Pharmacist 4 demonstrates this;

> We don't actually practice making medicines in the department anymore…that's a bit of a negative… It's become more patient-focused. So actually out there on the wards working with patients rather than in the department. And we've actually deskilled, which I'm not so sure is a good thing HP4

Within this quote, the implementation of technology into hospital pharmacy is appraised as a way in which the sector has been deskilled vis-a-vis medicines manufacturing. Within this, innovations which enable clinical work are posited as ways in which the activities of pharmacy have been reconfigured away from the central focus on medicines production, which characterised traditional pharmacy practice. This evaluation of innovation is notwithstanding the involvement of pharmacists in producing medicines through their involvement with clinical trials. Hence, although the work involved in making medicines has been modified (which is the root of Hospital Pharmacist Four's concern about deskilling), pharmacists involvement in clinical trials can be understood as their continued symbolic involvement in medicines manufacturing,

Hospital Pharmacist 4's evaluation of technology in hospital pharmacy, however, resonates with Novek's (2000) study of automated dispensing technology in three Canadian hospital pharmacies. In these three hospitals this technology, which was implemented in line with local medicines management and safety policies, is appraised as a means through which medications dispensing, as the core interest and work of pharmacy, is routinised in order to be delegated to pharmacy technical staff. In doing so, technology can act to shift the professional boundaries of pharmacy and pharmacy technician work and, as a result, was resisted by Novek's respondents.

Individual appraisal processes also involve locating the additional labour necessary for implementing innovations within the occupational demands and workloads of the given practice context. In their work on pharmacy robots, Barrett et al. (2011: 10) note that 'new routines in pharmacy work' had to be developed in order to overcome technical and mechanical difficulties with the technology. In this case, this new work was most frequently undertaken by pharmacy assistants in order to minimise the impact on pharmacists' core activities. In other cases, however, new technologies which necessitate a restructuring of everyday workloads are a central feature of the work of pharmacists and are, thus, appraised within the context of pharmacists' (as opposed to their support staff's) everyday activities. An example of this is provided by Hospital Pharmacist 4 who evaluated the value email technology in the context of pharmacists' everyday workload:

> One of the downsides is, I think, we're all burdened by email now. At one point you used to pick up the phone to communicate with somebody. Now, for example on Monday I was off and I came in one Tuesday to over 200 emails. And you can't actually manage to keep up with them HP4

This comment locates individual appraisal activities within workload management concerns and the contextual integration detailed in NPT. Here, the implementation of e-mail technology into everyday pharmacy work is understood to include increased labour which cannot easily be configured into everyday activities. This individual appraisal sits somewhat in opposition to more communal appraisals of communication technologies in pharmacy which email is assessed as a useful technology for pharmacy practice vis-à-vis patient safety and inter-professional communication (see Pohjanoksa-Mäntylä et al. 2008). The integration of email technology (as a means to communicate with other healthcare practitioners and patients) into everyday practice is appraised as a disruption of current communication practices. In this way, utilising e-mail technology generates additional labour with no apparent added value over traditional methods and so its capacity for contextual integration is limited.

3.5 Conclusion

In summary, pharmacy is a site of regular innovation where new practices, drugs and devices routinely reorganise work and relationships. Despite this, the process of implementing new technologies into community and hospital practice is under-researched in social sciences.

This chapter has argued that community and hospital pharmacists interact with different technologies in their everyday practice. Through the use of May and Finch's (2009) notion of coherence work, the chapter has shown how new technologies are made sense of through both formalised bureaucratic medicines management and pharmaceutical care policies and less discursive everyday practices. The divergence between the technologies of community and hospital pharmacy has been conceptualised as two epistemic groups of technologies- those of clinical work and those enabling clinical work. What both suggest, however, is the centrality of innovations to the reorganisation of pharmacy work around a more clinical focus. In the case of community pharmacy, this more clinical focus is argued to be enacted through testing and monitoring devices that construct individual patient risk profiles, which collectively construct a public health body, to then be partly managed by the pharmacist as a reconfigured public health practitioner. In the hospital setting, clinical work is enabled through technologies, such as dispensing robots and computers, which carry out the mundane tasks of previously dispensary-bound pharmacists. In doing so, pharmacists are less spatially-bound to the dispensary and increase their presence in more clinical work areas, namely the in-patient wards.

Although both of these groups of technologies are operationalised through formalised bureaucratic policies as improving patient health, improving medicines efficacy and assisting with auditing pharmacy services, May and Finch's (2009) NPT provides useful constructs for analysing the evaluative work which is carried out at the level of everyday practice. Within this, the notions of 'reflexive monitoring' and 'contextual integration' have been shown to be useful sensitising tools for conceptualising this process. These constructs have been mobilised here to show the ways in which new technologies may fail to be normalised into everyday pharmacy practice when the current structure of practice is incompatible with the additional work created by these technologies.

Elsewhere, case studies of technologies in pharmacy practice have shed light on technologically-mediated professional reorganisation (for example, Abarca et al. 2006; Barrett et al. 2011; Foster 1992; Motulsky et al. 2008). Despite these examples, STS research in this field is comparatively sparse and future research would benefit from a consideration of pharmacy as a site of innovation and professional boundary work vis-à-vis new technological artefacts and practices.

References

Abarca, J., Colon, L., Wang, V., Malone, D., Murphy, J., & Armstrong, E. (2006). Evaluation of the performance of drug-drug interaction screening software in community and hospital pharmacies. *Journal of managed care pharmacy, JMCP, 12*(5), 383–389.

Anderson, S. (2001). The historical context of pharmacy. In K. Taylor & G. Harding (Eds.), *Pharmacy practice* (pp. 3–31). London: Taylor and Francis.

Anderson, S. (2007). Community pharmacy and public health in Great Britain, 1936 to 2006: How a phoenix rose from the ashes. *Journal of Epidemiology and Community Health, 61*(10), 844–848.

Armstrong, D. (1995). The rise of surveillance medicine. *Sociology of Health & Illness, 17*(3), 393–404.

Audit Commission. (2001). *A spoonful of sugar: Medicines management in NHS hospitals*. London: Audit Commission.

Bajramovic, J., Emmerton, L., & Tett, S. E. (2004). Perceptions around concordance: Focus groups and semi-structured interviews conducted with consumers, Pharmacists and General Practitioners. *Health Expectations, 7*(3), 221–234.

Barber, N. (2001). Pharmaceutical care and medicines management: Is there a difference? *Pharmacy World & Science, 23*(6), 210–211.

Barber, N. (2005). The pharmaceutical gaze: The defining feature of pharmacy? *The Pharmaceutial Journal, 275*, 78.

Barrett, M., Oborn, E., Orlikowski, W. J., & Yates, J. A. (2011). Reconfiguring boundary relations: Robotic innovations in pharmacy work. *Organization Science,*. doi:10.1287/o rsc.1100.0639.

Bhakta, H. (2010). Moving from the community to hospital, *Tomorrow's Pharmacist*. http://www.pjonline.com/tomorrows- pharmacist/career_options/hospital/move_from_community Accessed April 2012.

Birenbaum, A. (1990). *In the shadow of medicine*. New York: General Hall.

Cerulo, K. A. (2009). Nonhumans in social interaction. *Annual Review of Sociology, 35*, 531–552.

Cooper, R., Bissell, P., & Wingfield, J. (2009). 'Islands' and 'doctor's tool': The ethical significance of isolation and subordination in UK community pharmacy. *Health, 13*(3), 297–316.

Cribb, A. (2011). *Involvement, shared decision-making and medicines*. London: Royal Pharmaceutical Society.

Department of Health and Royal Pharmaceutical Society of Great Britain. (1992). *Pharmaceutical care: The future for community pharmacy*. London: Royal Pharmaceutical Society of Great Britain.

Dingwall, R., & Wilson, E. (1995). Is pharmacy really an incomplete profession? *Perspectives on Social Problems, 7*, 111–128.

Eaton, G., & Webb, B. (1979). Boundary encroachment: Pharmacists in the clinical setting. *Sociology of Health & Illness, 1*(1), 69–89.

Edmunds, J., & Calnan, M. (2001). The reprofessionalisation of community pharmacy? An exploration of attitudes to extended roles for community pharmacists amongst pharmacists and general practitioners in the United Kingdom. *Social Science and Medicine, 53*(7), 943–955.

Finch, T. (2008). Teledermatology for chronic disease management: Coherence and normalization. *Chronic illness, 4*(2), 127–134.

Fleck, L. (1979). *Genesis and development of a scientific fact*. Chicago: Chicago University Press.

Foster, R. M. (1992). *The Computerisation of Community Pharmacy*. Academic Unpublished Thesis: The University of Aston, Birmingham.

Franx, G., Oud, M., De Lange, J., Wensing, M., & Grol, R. (2012). Implementing a stepped care approach in primary care. Results of a qualitative study. *Implementation Science, 7*(1), 8–21.

General Pharmaceutical Council. (2012). Inappropriate touching during examination in pharmacy consultation room leads to warning for pharmacist. *The Pharmaceutial Journal, 288*(7690), 122.

Grint, K., & Woolgar, S. (1997). *The machine at work*. Cambridge: Polity Press.

Hall, N. (1970). *Report of the working party on the hospital pharmaceutical service*. London: HMSO.

Harding, G., & Taylor, K. (1997). Responding to change: the case of community pharmacy in Great Britain. *Sociology of Health & Illness, 19*(5), 547–560.

Heath, C., Luff, P., & Svensson, M. S. (2003). Technology and medical practice. *Sociology of Health & Illness, 25*(3), 75–96.

Hutchby, I. (2003). Affordances and the analysis of technologically mediated interaction. *Sociology, 37*(3), 581–589.

Keller, D. M. (2009). From shotgun to gatling gun: Multi-barrelled approach to cancer treatment. *Oncology Times UK, 6*(5), 17.

Korica, M., & Molloy, E. (2010). Making sense of professional identities: Stories of medical professionals and new technologies. *Human Relations, 63*(12), 1879–1901.

Levitt, R. (1976). *The reorganised national health service*. London: Croom Helm Ltd.

Makowsky, M. J., Schindel, T. J., Rosenthal, M., Campbell, K., Tsuyuki, R. T., & Madill, H. M. (2009). Collaboration between pharmacists, physicians and nurse practitioners: A qualitative investigation of working relationships in the inpatient medical setting. *Journal of Interprofessional Care, 23*(2), 169–184.

May, C., & Finch, T. (2009). Implementing, embedding, and integrating practices: An outline of normalization process theory. *Sociology, 43*(3), 535–554.

Mclaughlin, J., & Webster, A. (1998). Rationalising knowledge: IT systems, professional identities and power. *The Sociological Review, 46*(4), 781–802.

Motulsky, A., Winslade, N., Tamblyn, R., & Sicotte, C. (2008). The impact of electronic prescribing on the professionalization of community pharmacists: A qualitative study of pharmacists perception. *Journal of Pharmacy and Pharmaceutical Sciences, 11*(1), 131–146.

Novek, J. (2000). Hospital pharmacy automation: collective mobility or collective control? *Social Science and Medicine, 51*(4), 491–503.

Nuffield Committee of Inquiry into Pharmacy. (1986). *Pharmacy: A report to the Nuffield Foundation*. London: Nuffield Foundation.

Pohjanoksa-Mäntylä, M. K., Kulovaara, H., Bell, J. S., Enäkoski, M., & Airaksinen, M. S. (2008). Email medication counseling services provided by Finnish Community pharmacies. *The Annals of pharmacotherapy, 42*(12), 1782–1790.

Prout, A. (1996). Actor-network theory, technology and medical sociology: An illustrative analysis of the metered dose inhaler. *Sociology of Health & Illness, 18*(2), 198–219.

Rappert, B. (2003). Technologies, texts and possibilities: A reply to Hutchby. *Sociology, 37*(3), 565–580.

Rose, N. (2007). Molecular biopolitics, somatic ethics and the spirit of biocapital. *Social Theory and Health, 5*(1), 3–29.

Royal Pharmaceutical Society of Great Britain. (1995). *Pharmacy in a new age; the new horizon*. London: Royal Pharmaceutical Society of Great Britain.

Shrank, W., Avorn, J., Rolon, C., & Shekelle, P. (2007a). Effect of content and format of prescription drug labels on readability, understanding, and medication use: A systematic review. *The Annals of Pharmacotherapy, 41*(5), 783–801.

Shrank, W. H., Agnew-Blais, J., Choudhry, N. K., Wolf, M. S., Kesselheim, A. S., Avorn, J., et al. (2007b). The variability and quality of medication container labels. *Archives of Internal Medicine, 167*(16), 1760–1765.

So, J. (2010). Improving the quality of oral chemotherapy services using home care. *European Journal of Cancer Care, 19*, 35–39.

Steyer, T. E., Ragucci, K. R., Pearson, W. S., & Mainous, A. G. (2004). The role of pharmacists in the delivery of influenza vaccinations. *Vaccine, 22*(8), 1001–1006.

Stone, P., & Curtis, S. J. (2002). *Pharmacy practice* (3rd ed.). London: The Pharmaceutical Press.

Taylor, D. (2005). The apothecary's return? A brief look at pharmacy's future', in Anderson, S. (ed.) *Making Medicines: A Brief History of Pharmacy and Pharmaceuticals*. London: The Pharmaceutical Press. pp 283–299

Zetka, J. R. (2001). Occupational divisions of labor and their technology politics: The case of surgical scopes and gastrointestinal medicine. *Social Forces, 79*(4), 1495–1520.

Chapter 4
Patients' Perceptions of a Home Telecare System

Mohammadreza Rahimpour, Nigel H. Lovell, Branko G. Celler and John McCormick

Abstract *Goal:* To identify any major factors that could affect patients' perceptions of a Home Telecare Management System (HTMS) and use the findings to contribute to development of a theoretical framework for patient acceptance of HTMS. *Materials and methods:* Ten Focus Group Interviews (FGIs) were conducted with patients suffering from congestive heart failure (CHF), chronic obstructive pulmonary disease (COPD), or both, from seven different ethnic groups in Sydney. Six key discussion points were used to conduct the FGIs. The participants were shown a video demonstrating the HTMS and its operation, followed by the demonstration of an HTMS prototype. The participants, who had no prior experience with the HTMS, were then asked questions to access their perceptions in potentially real situations. The discussions were audio-taped and content analysis performed. *Results:* Four major themes and 16 sub-themes were identified. The themes were: intention to use the HTMS, the impact of the HTMS on patients' health management, concerns associated with using the HTMS, and the impact of the HTMS on healthcare services.

Keywords Home telecare • Perception • Acceptance • Self-efficacy • Technophobia • Ageing • Chronic disease

This chapter originally appeared in *International Journal of Medical Informatics,* Vol. 77 (2008) pp. 486–498 and is reprinted here by courtesy of Elsevier. © 2007 Elsevier Ireland Ltd. Please note: This chapter includes a shorter version of the article abstract as originally published.

M. Rahimpour · N. H. Lovell (✉) · B. G. Celler · J. McCormick
University of New South Wales, Sydney, Australia
e-mail: n.lovell@unsw.edu.au

4.1 Introduction

Implementation of a Home Telecare Management System (HTMS) (Lovell et al. 2002; Celler et al. 2003) may be associated with user resistance. This may be particularly important when technical innovation is applied to managing chronic healthcare in elderly patients who are unaccustomed to modern technology. Patients' perceptions of home telecare are likely to influence its acceptability (Palmas et al. 2006; Demiris 2000). Ignoring the human side of such a technology innovation may limit its usefulness and delay proper decision-making. Therefore, the study of patients' perceptions can contribute to the eventual success of the HTMS programs.

In this trial a pre-production prototype of a HTMS that is now manufactured by MedCare Systems Pty. Ltd. (Sydney, NSW, Australia) was used. The HTMS was designed to record clinical indicators of a patient's health status and to provide feedback to patients including medication reminders and measurement scheduling (Celler et al. 2003). It incorporated an extensive suite of clinical measurements including a wireless weight scale, single lead electrocardiogram, blood pressure cuff, spirometer, temperature probe, and pulse oximeter. A comprehensive suite of Webenabled tools facilitated patient management by the care team.

Most published studies of subjective aspects of telemedicine applications have investigated patients/providers' satisfaction/perception after receiving telemedicine services (Palmas et al. 2006; Demiris 2000; Liu et al. 2007; Abrams and Geier 2006; Chumbler et al. 2004; Demiris et al. 2004; Finkelstein et al. 2004; Chae et al. 2001; Dick et al. 1999; Mekhjian et al. 1999). Most studies have attempted to explore how patients rate specific aspects of telemedicine services. Finkelstein et al. (2004) in a randomised case control study reported that all subjects (congestive heart failure (CHF), chronic obstructive pulmonary disease (COPD), and chronic wound care patients) were satisfied with their standard home health care and their satisfaction increased with an increasing level of home telecare intervention. Chumbler et al. (2004) in a case control study compared health related outcomes of frail elders who received home teleheatlh and those who received no intervention. They reported that the majority of 111 older patients, who received home telehealth intervention felt more secure, found the system easy to use and helpful in managing their chronic illnesses (hypertension, diabetes, heart disease, and respiratory disease). Demiris et al. (2004) explored the perceptions of seniors in regard to 'smart home' technology installed and operated in their homes by conducting three focus groups. Although, they reported overall positive attitude towards devices and sensors, concerns were expressed about the user-friendliness of the devices, lack of human response and the need for tailoring the training to older learners.

Using qualitative methods, Agrell et al. (2000), Finkelstein et al. (1999), Mair et al. (2000), and (Whitten and Collins 1998; Whitten et al. 1997) studied patients' perceptions of home telenursing after experiencing the system. Generally, they found that patients' perceptions were positive. Demiris et al. (2001), in a case controlled trial, studied elderly patients' perceptions of home telecare using a questionnaire. Patients were assessed both before and after using the system. The results indicated that the experimental group generally expressed more positive perceptions after experiencing the system than the control group. Brignell et al. (2007) recently reviewed the existing literature to identify strategies for application of telemedicine in geriatric medical practice, who concluded that there is evidence to suggest that a number of telemedicine systems can be applied effectively in geriatric medicine. They also pointed out that patient satisfaction has been generally reported as high, and advised caution in this regard due to the insufficient number of robust studies in the literature.

It is worth noting that previous studies about patients' perceptions of home telecare have used different technological approaches that tended to be based around home telenursing and/or teleconsultation using video conferencing (Demiris 2000; Liu et al. 2007; Agrell et al. 2000; Finkelstein et al. 1999; Mair et al. 2000; Whitten and Collins 1998). However, the technology used in the HTMS involves active management strategies, including scheduling patient measurements and medications.

Several conceptualisations of patients' perceptions of home telecare have been introduced by different investigators (Demiris 2000; Agrell et al. 2000; Whitten et al. 1997). Since the HTMS is not the same type of home telecare used in previous studies, there are factors identified in these studies, which were considered inappropriate for inclusion in this study unless some modifications were considered. For example, the HTMS does not include teleconsultation, therefore, "video consideration" (Agrell et al. 2000), "factors related to the conduct of a virtual visit" (Demiris 2000) and "patients' views of the implications of telenursing for their healthcare" (Whitten et al. 1997) categories are not applicable in this study. Likewise, "physical presence considerations" (Agrell et al. 2000), which referred to the impact of home telecare on physical presence of the medical practitioner or other medical staff (a health care worker) and its relationship with patients' satisfaction and "patients' perceptions of communications issues" (Whitten et al. 1997) are not relevant to the HTMS.

It was theorised that patients' perceptions of the HTMS could be categorised as shown in Table 4.1. Since it was intended to propose a model for patients' acceptance of the HTMS (Rahimpour 2006) based on the Technology Acceptance Model (TAM) of Davis (1989, 1986), TAM factors were incorporated into the conceptual framework.

In response to the paucity of robust qualitative studies of patients' perceptions of HTMS, an important and new aspect of the study is its integration of TAM in the research design (conceptual framework). Indeed, we consider a comprehensive protocol, such as we used in this study to be vital for investigation of patients' perceptions of HTMS.

The TAM introduced by Davis (1986) has been well-researched in the area of information systems over nearly two decades and supported by many studies. There is evidence that the TAM has been successful in predicting usage across a variety of new technologies (King and Jun 2006; Chang 1998; Szajna 1996; Igbaria 1993). The TAM provides a general explanation of the determinants of

Table 4.1 Conceptual framework for patients' perceptions of HTMS

TAM related factors	Overall attitude toward the HTMS
	Perceived usefulness
	Perceived ease of use
	Intention to use
Impact on patients' health status management	Impact on patients' health status management by themselves
	Impact on patients' knowledge and education about their health status
	Impact on participation of patients in their health status management
	Impact on patients' health status management by physicians
Factors related to the use of HTMS	Confidentiality
Impact of the HTMS on health care	Access to health care
Cost and time	The impact of the system on health care cost
	The impact of the system on patients' time

computer acceptance and explains computer usage behaviour in a wide range of computer user domains.

In the TAM, user acceptance is evaluated by assessing users' beliefs, attitudes, intentions, and actual usage behaviour. As shown in Fig. 4.1, according to the TAM, a user's attitude toward using the system is a major determinant of whether or not he or she actually uses it. Attitude (A) is defined as positive or negative feelings toward the information technology (IT). Behavioural intention (BI) is defined as "a person's subjective probability that he will perform some behaviour" (Fishbein and Ajzen 1975). BI to use a system is modelled as a function of attitude and usefulness, which determines the actual use.

Attitude toward the system is determined by a function of two beliefs, PU and PEOU. Perceived usefulness (PU) is "the degree to which a person believes that using a particular system would enhance his/her job performance" (Davis 1989). Perceived ease of use (PEOU) is "the degree to which a person believes that using a particular system would be free of effort" (Davis 1989).

In the HTMS context, attitude is the degree of evaluative affect that a patient associates with using the HTMS in management of her/his health condition. Perceived usefulness is the degree to which a patient believes that using the HTMS

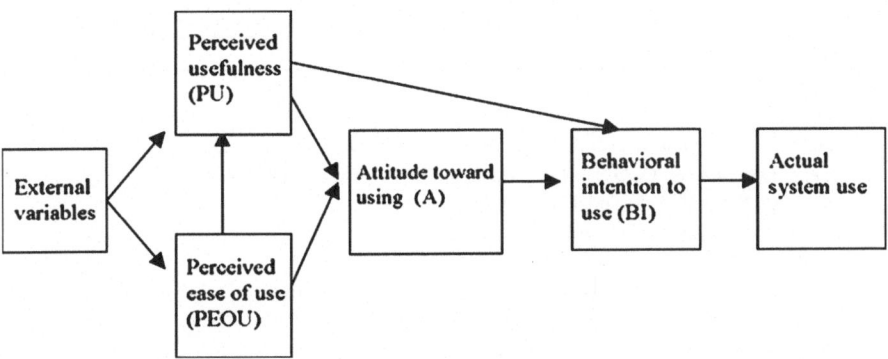

Fig. 4.1 The technology acceptance model (TAM) from Davis et al. (1989), p. 985)

would facilitate the management of her or his health condition. Ease of use is the degree to which a patient believes that using an HTMS would be free of effort. Intention to use refers to a patient's subjective probability that she or he will use the HTMS in managing her/his health condition (Rahimpour 2006).

In addition, other factors such as the impact of the HTMS on patients' health management, cost and time and accessibility to healthcare which previous studies [e.g. (Demiris et al. 2004; Woods et al. 1999)] have shown affect patients' perceptions of home telecare, were included.

Earlier studies [e.g. (Finkelstein et al. 1999; Demiris et al. 2001)] have shown that in home telecare contexts, which included teleconsultations or virtual visits, patients had concerns about 'confidentiality' and lack of 'physical presence' of a health care worker. Although the HTMS does not include virtual visits or teleconsultation, patients' information is stored and transferred by the system. Therefore, it was considered worthwhile to include these two factors in the conceptual framework. Finally, "training" was incorporated because the target group consisted of elderly patients with chronic disease, for whom training to use the HTMS may be important.

An interview schedule based on the conceptual framework (Table 4.2) was developed to address the objectives of this study which is to identify any major factors that could affect patients' acceptance of a HTMS and to use the findings to contribute to development of a theoretical framework for patient acceptance of HTMS.

4.2 Methods

4.2.1 Sample

In order to account for the cultural diversity in Australia, patients from different ethnic backgrounds suffering from either, CHF, COPD, or both, were invited to

Table 4.2 Research protocol for the focus group interviews (topic guideline)

Categories/questions
TAM related factors
Overall attitude toward the HTMS: Q. Overall, do you like the system? If so, what do you like about the system? (Demiris et al. 2000)
Perceived usefulness: Q. Overall do you think the system would be useful for you? What possible advantages and disadvantages do you foresee?
Perceived ease of use
Perceived ease of use: Q. How did you perceive the system in terms of whether it is easy or difficult to use? Q. Do you think other patients' who have similar conditions to you would be able to operate the system?
Perceived self-efficacy of using the system: Q. If the system was available how are you confident that you could use the system?
Intention to use: Q. If the system were available, would you be interested in using it? Q. Do you think other patients who have similar conditions to you would be interested in using the system? (Demiris et al. 2000)
The impact on patients' health management
The impact on patients' health status management by themselves: Q. Do you think the system would improve your health management by yourself? If so, how? Q. Do you think the system would improve your knowledge and education about your health status management?
The impact on patients' health status management by the physicians: Q. Do you think the system would affect health management by your medical practitioner? If so how?
Factors related to the use of HTMS
Confidentiality (Agrell et al. 2000): Q. Are you concerned about the confidentiality of the data in the system?
Lack of physical presence (Agrell et al. 2000): Q. By using the system you take your measurements yourself and part of your health status management will be performed through the system. That may decrease your face-to-face visits with your doctor, are you concerned about that? What do you think?
Training: Q. What kind of training you think would suit you?
The impact on health care services
The impact on the access to health care (Demiris et al. 2000): Q. Do you think the system will affect access to health care? If so, how?
The impact on the use of health care services: Q. Do you think the system will affect the number of medical practitioner visits, emergency department visits and hospital admissions? If so, how?
Cost and time (Demiris et al. 2000)
The impact of the HTMS on health care cost: Q. Do you think this system will save money? If so, how?
The impact of the HTMS on patients' time: Q. Do you think the system will save your time? If so, how?

participate in this study. Studies were conducted with institutional ethics approval (#03/04) from the South East Health Human Research Ethics Committee. Multicultural Health Unit experts from the South East Sydney Area Health Service were consulted, and a decision made to initially involve seven different ethnic groups. Using databases from the Prince of Wales Hospital, Sydney, 10 focus groups which met inclusion criteria were identified. Focus group sessions were scheduled separately for each ethnic group. Four of the groups comprised members identified as Anglo/Celtic participants; the other groups comprised participants identified as Italian, Chinese, Assyrian, Russian, Greek and South Pacific Islander. This was considered representative of the part of Sydney from which the sample was drawn.

Subjects:

1. had to be more than 40 years old;
2. had to have a primary diagnosis of CHF, class II to IV of NYHA (New York Heart Association), chronic obstructive pulmonary disease (COPD), or both;
3. had to be members of one of the major ethnic communities in the south east area of Sydney;
4. had to be able to read, write, and speak in their native languages;
5. had to be mentally able to understand the consent form.

A letter, explaining the purpose of the study was provided in English and the appropriate language for non-English background participants, was delivered to each patient. After 1 week, patients were contacted and the relevant health workers explained the purpose of the study and invited them to participate. Since the target subjects were elderly patients with chronic conditions, it was predicted that the "refusal to participate" rate would be considerable. Therefore, for each putative focus group, 12 patients were contacted to achieve an expected minimum group size of six participants. Approximately 78 % of those approached agreed to participate, although, of those who agreed some were unable to attend, due to ill health. Overall, 64 % (a total of 77 volunteers) participated in the Focus Group Interviews (FGIs), with group size varying from 6 to 12. Patients' ages ranged from 50 to 90 years, with mean and median ages of 71 years and 1 months and 71 years, respectively.

4.2.2 Procedures

Ten focus groups were conducted with the first author acting as a moderator and a trained research assistant as a facilitator. When the members of the focus group were from non-English speaking backgrounds, a relevant health worker/interpreter with the same ethnicity was also included as a facilitator to interpret and assist in conducting the FGI. The interpreter also received the

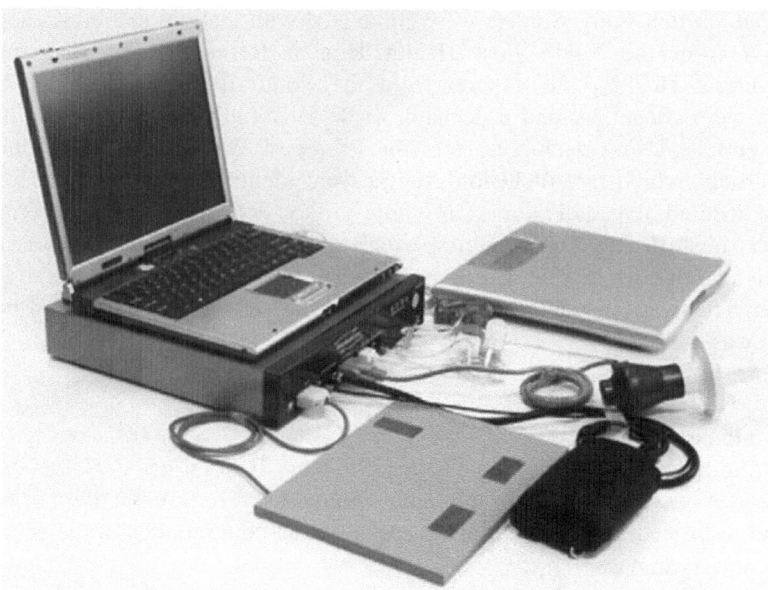

Fig. 4.2 The home telecare patient unit as demonstrated in the focus groups, showing the computer screen with clinical measurement unit underneath and the various peripherals used for physiological recording. These include a wireless weight scale, single lead electrocardiogram, blood pressure cuff, spirometer, and pulse oximeter

necessary training. All instructions were translated into the relevant languages and displayed on large sheets during the sessions, as for the English-speaking groups. To maintain anonymity, the participants were given a label with two letters: N and F. N was the position of the participants from the right side of the moderator and F was the label for the focus group. For example, N1F1 was the first participant at the right side of the moderator and F1 was the first conducted focus group.

The purpose and the procedure of the focus group interviewing were described in general terms at the beginning of each FGI. All participants agreed to have the interviews recorded. It was also emphasised that their responses would be strictly confidential. Then, the participants were shown a videotape in which a model patient in the age range of participants demonstrated the functions of the HTMS, in a room consistent with a home environment. The range of clinical measurements that the HTMS could provide (e.g.; recording clinical indicators of a patient's health status such as blood pressure, spirometry, temperature, weight, heart rate, ECG and providing feedback to patients including medication reminders and measurement scheduling) was shown on the video. All HTMS instructions in the video were translated into the relevant languages and were displayed on large sheets during the video demonstration, to ensure consistency with the English-speaking groups. The video demonstration was developed by the first author with collaboration of the Educational Development & Technology Centre of the University of New South Wales. A copy of the video is held by the University.

After the video demonstration an HTMS prototype was demonstrated which is shown in Fig. 4.2 (Celler et al. 2003) and patients' questions were answered without any favouring of the system by the first author. Then, the participants, who had no prior experience of the HTMS, were asked questions to access their perceptions in potentially real situations. Each group discussion was conducted for approximately 90 min. The end point of each discussion was when the researcher perceived that the six major topics, as listed in the research protocol (Table 4.2) were exhausted, no new information in the major topics had been revealed for a while, or themes were being repeated (Ritchie 2001; Fontana and Frey 1994). The discussions were audio-taped. In addition, notes were taken to document the non-verbal interactions and general content of the discussion.

Although it may be argued that it would have been desirable for participants to have experienced an actual HTMS, this would have required a much greater expenditure of time and money. Perhaps more importantly, one of the main purposes of the study was to inform development and implementation of the HTMS. Consistent with this, Davis (1986) argued that it is not vital for a fully developed system to be employed at the prototype stage. Consequently, a video demonstration and prototype HTMS were employed in this study. Moreover, it has consistently been found that people develop relatively stable beliefs about their capabilities to perform tasks (self-efficacy) by vicarious learning (Bandura 1997).

4.3 Analysis

Audio-tapes in English were transcribed soon after each FGI by the first author and those in other languages by the relevant health workers. The transcripts were checked several times against the original tapes until they were accepted as accurate. Indicators of affective states such as laughing were also included in transcription. In order to analyse the comments, after each FGI, the moderator and facilitator met to discuss the data and attempt to identify the overall trends and patterns that emerged. First, the key concepts of the comments were identified, and then grouped into categories (CA). Based on the categories, several sub-themes (STn) and themes (Tn) were then identified. The data were also reviewed by two independent researchers to validate the categorised responses. A list of core themes and sub-themes were identified by the iterative process of carefully reading the transcripts. Four major themes and 16 sub-themes were identified from the participants' comments. The themes are: intention to use the HTMS (T1), the impact of the HTMS on patients' health management (T2), concerns associated with using the HTMS (T3), and the impact of the HTMS on healthcare services (T4). The themes and sub-themes are presented in Table 4.3.

Table 4.3 Summary of themes, sub-themes, and categories that resulted from the FGI analysis

Themes	Sub-themes	Categories
Intention to use the HTMS (T1)	Overall attitude toward the HTMS (ST1)	Positive attitude toward the system (CA1)
		Negative attitude toward the system (CA2)
	Perceived usefulness (ST2)	It is convenient to have HTMS available (CA3)
		HTMS gives peace of mind (CA4)
		HTMS reduces patients' feeling of being alone (CA5)
		HTMS provide early warning of health status deterioration (CA6)
		HTMS reduces cost (CA7)
		For patients
		For government
		HTMS saves time (CA8)
		For patients
		For physicians
	Perceived ease of use (ST3)	HTMS is easy to use (CA9)
		HTMS is not easy to use (CA10)
	Intention to use (ST4)	Intended to use (CA11)
		Not intended to use (CA12)
	HTMS self-efficacy (ST5)	Thinking being able to use the system (CA13) Thinking not being able to use the system (CA14)
	HTMS anxiety (ST6)	Feeling anxious when thinking about using the system (CA15)
		Feeling not anxious when thinking about using the system (CA16)
The impact on patients' health management (T2)	The HTMS may improve patients' health management by themselves (ST7)	The HTMS improves patients' knowledge (CA17)
		Inform patients about their health status more often and more accurate than what they do now (CA18)

(Continued)

	The HTMS may improve patients' health management by the medical doctor (ST8)	Empower patients to improve their self-care (CA19)
		Play more active role in their management (CA20)
		Improve patients' compliance (CA21)
		Providing updated health measurements for medical doctor (CA22)
		Providing more accurate measurements, more often to medical doctor (CA23)
		Better decision making by physicians (CA24)
		Facilitate exchange of information related to patients' health between different level of health care providers (CA25)
Concerns associated with using the HTMS (T3)	Confidentiality (ST9)	Misuse of confidential information (CA26)
	Lack of physical presence of medical doctor (ST10)	Like to see medical doctor face to face (CA27)
	Equipment reliability (ST11)	Concern about reliability of the HTMS (CA28)
	HTMS support (ST12)	Concern about clinical support of the HTMS (CA29)
	Cost (ST13)	Concern about technical support of the HTMS (CA30)
		Concern about the cost of the HTMS (CA31)
	Training programs for the patients who are going to use the HTMS (ST14)	Elderly patients may need more time to be taught how to use the HTMS (CA32)
		Some elderly people may benefit from individualised training programs (CA33)
The impact on health care services (T4)	The impact on access to health care (ST15)	The impact on access to health care for elderly homebound patients with chronic disease (CA34)
		The impact on access to health care for remote areas (CA35)
		The impact on access to health care for metropolitan areas (CA36)
	The impact on use of health care services (ST16)	Decrease in emergency department utilisation and hospital admissions (CA37)
		Decrease the number of medical visits (CA38)

4.4 Results

4.4.1 Intention to Use the HTMS

4.4.1.1 Overall Attitude Toward the HTMS

Participants' attitudes were generally positive about the HTMS (CA1). Most stated that they liked the system. They frequently referred to different aspects of their perceptions of HTMS when responding to questions and expressed positive attitudes. For example, some pointed out that by using HTMS they could become more aware of their health conditions and have improved peace of mind:

> I really like it because I get to know whether my body is functioning well from the daily measurements that are shown on the computer at the comfort of my own home. This means that I don't have to worry about my health as much.

4.4.1.2 Perceived Usefulness

The majority of participants agreed that using the HTMS could be more convenient (CA3) than other methods of health care delivery. Less travelling, time saved, and fewer medical visits were identified as useful aspects of the HTMS. One participant said:

> To see my doctor can be three hours of wait at times. With this system, it will be much easier for me… I think this system is really convenient. I don't need to visit my doctor as often if I have this system installed at home.

Most participants pointed to positive psychological aspects of using the HTMS and agreed that it could give them peace of mind (CA4). Being informed about one's health status, and being regularly aware of the results was the most prominent aspect of the HTMS, stated as providing peace of mind, for example:

> … I think it will make people more relaxed because they know exactly what's happening to them. If you are not feeling too well, you can go back on and recheck your status. It is going to definitely keep a lot of people less worried, which will be beneficial for them. By cutting down the stress, it takes their fears away… not all of it but at least some of it.

Some participants referred to their loneliness, and stated that having such a system at home for elderly people, who live alone, would reduce their anxiety of being alone (CA5), for example:

> … I live on my own with no one around me, not a neighbour, a dog…not even a cat. I like it (system) because I am on my own. Health wise I feel like I am not on my own with this system.

Participants agreed that the HTMS could warn patients at an early stage of health deterioration (CA6), and they could intervene accordingly using feedback provided by the system.

Although many agreed with the concept of cost saving, they generally added conditionally that the system should be provided in a way that would be affordable to consumers. The main expected reasons for cost savings were: less travelling, fewer hospital admissions and reduced number of visits to medical practitioners. One of the participants argued:

> ...people living in the remote areas, not necessarily in a rural area, including suburban areas, probably have to travel 20–30 km to come in and see the doctor because they live on the property, in a farm or whatever... the doctor can monitor your health (using the system). If the patient is not ill, he can monitor him without having to say, I want to see you next week. The patient doesn't have to travel frequently to see the doctor as he has got all his recordsand data...

Generally, although some participants expressed some concerns about the HTMS (confidentiality, lack of physical presence of a health care worker, equipment reliability, adequate HTMS technical support) most perceived the HTMS as a useful mode of healthcare delivery (ST2). The participants noted different aspects of the HTMS as reasons for their positive perceptions, for example, providing feedback and awareness of current health conditions, having playing a preventative role and providing accurate and up-to-date health information. Other comments related to peace of mind, saving expenses and time and reducing loneliness and convenience.

4.4.1.3 Perceived Ease of Use

On the whole, participants' opinions about ease of use (ST3) of the HTMS were extremely varied, ranging from very easy to very difficult. Some participants agreed that the system was easy to use (CA9). For example, one said:

> ...From the demonstration shown in the video, it seems that it is not difficult to follow and it looks quite simple and easy

On the other hand, some participants disagreed (CA10), for example:

> ...This system looks a bit complicated...I think our main problem is that it may be difficult to operate. That's what I've picked out.

4.4.1.4 Intention to Use

Most participants expressed willingness to use the system in managing their health if it were available in the future (CA11), for example:

> ...I think it is a splendid idea, I will go for it if it comes out in the market. Because, I live alone and I would be very happy to have something monitoring me.

4.4.1.5 HTMS Self-Efficacy

HTMS self-efficacy is conceptualised as the judgment of one's capability to use the HTMS (Rahimpour 2006). Although the majority of the patients stated they thought that they could use the system (CA13), however, a considerable number of participants did not think that they could use the system independently (CA14) and expressed low levels of confidence for using the system.

> This is a very difficult system. We need to know how to operate it... It is a wonderful system but it's impossible to keep all of this information in the head.

Some participants believed it would be too difficult for elderly people to learn.

> ...I couldn't even turn it on. I mean, I am at this stage of my life where I am not going to learn it. Why would I bother to learn it...I think it is impossible for older people to understand how the system works. For older people it is very hard to understand which buttons they need to push. They could not even understand how a VCR is connected to a TV. For older people it's impossible to operate it...the system is very good, but we are in a condition that we can't even do the simplest things. I know that I wouldn't be able to do it.

4.4.1.6 HTMS Anxiety

HTMS anxiety is conceptualised as a negative psychological reaction that impedes a positive adaptation to and creative use of the HTMS (Rahimpour 2006). At least one patient in each focus group referred to herself or himself as the elderly people who feared and avoided to be confronted with modern technology such as HTMS.

> ...we have not grown up with computers,...you only have to look at the level of resistance from older people using ATMs in the banks. A lot of old people when confronted with such a system, freeze up, as it is complicated for them.... something they fear.

Some patients perceived the system as a computer and expressed their computer anxiety, despite being informed they did not need any computer knowledge to use the HTMS, and it is not a PC. They viewed the HTMS as a computer due to the similar physical appearance (CA15). For example:

> I have never had anything to do with computer, and I take that all of these use computers...I don't know anything about computers...I like the system, but first of all, it is very hard to use it. I don't know how to use computers. I don't know what will happen to the computer if I press the wrong button.

4.4.2 The Impact on Patients' Health Management

4.4.2.1 The HTMS Improves Patients' Health Management by Themselves

Participants stated that the general description, progress and management of CHF and COPD, available in the system, would improve their knowledge about their health problems (CA17).

> ... a very important point is that you learn about your disease, what the causes are and how to manage them. It clarifies many questions in your mind... not only that but you also learn, whether you get better or worse.

Several patients stated that most of the time they were not aware of their health measurements, suffering from a lack of adequate and on time information about their health conditions. They agreed that by using the system they would be provided with more accurate and more frequent information about their health conditions (CA18). For example:

> Of course! Without proper measurements, we can only guess our blood pressure, heart rate etc., which are not reliable. We can take our measurement by this system everyday. If we have accurate information about our conditions it helps a lot... we can't just guess and delay the necessary treatment.

Participants agreed that the HTMS could empower patients to manage their health conditions better than they did currently (CA19), for example:

> ... It helps to manage my condition much better...I'd rather do it (taking measurements) myself than to go to the doctor every time to get tested.

Most participants believed that by using the HTMS they would play a more active role in their health management (CA20), for example:

> ...I have been asked by my family doctor to record my daily lung function test results because of my asthma condition, but I always forget to measure. With the assistance of this system installed at home, I am able to get proper measurements more often and see how I am going. If my asthma got worse I would look at the guideline which my doctor has given me and do something about it before ending up into hospital.

The scheduler/reminder system was appreciated by most of the participants as a useful aspect that could improve patient compliance (CA21), particularly for those who needed to take several medications, for example:

> ... I have problems with my eyes and also a severe arthritis. I have to take too many medications, and sometimes I forget to take them on time. This system can help me remember to take my medications on time.

4.4.2.2 The HTMS Improves Patient's Health Management by Medical Doctors

The concept that the HTMS can improve patients' health management by medical doctors (ST8) was mentioned by several participants. One said:

> With this system the doctor can review my condition regularly and if I am not well the doctor will have a complete picture of my condition. It would be a very big help.

Many participants agreed that the system would help the physicians to manage their health status better by providing up-to-date information (CA22), for example:

> ... the doctor can check my measurements every day. It's better to check them through the system every day than having to visit the doctor once a month. In that way, he would be able to have a better idea about my condition.

They also agreed that the HTMS provides more reliable information, more often to practitioners (CA23), for example:

... This system provides a more accurate description about my conditions, because I take the measurements at my home where I am more comfortable than my doctor surgery.

The issue of the doctor's decision being based on a limited number of measurements (CA24) was raised by some patients.

Sometimes it is not reliable if the prescription is made based on just one measurement taken from the doctor's surgery... sometimes when the doctor takes my blood pressure, it may be high initially and then, after several hours, it would return to normal. Without this system the doctor would not know the true readings.

Several participants believed the HTMS would facilitate exchange of information related to patients' health between different level of health care providers such as general practitioners and specialists (CA25).

... so with the system like this they will be able to send the data to each other (such as; general practitioner and specialist) quickly.

4.4.3 Concerns

4.4.3.1 Confidentiality

The majority of participants agreed that they were not concerned about confidentiality related to the HTMS provided that access to the health information would be limited to relevant medical doctors. One said:

... I have no concerns really... confidentiality doesn't worry me at all... frankly, it's not important to me, as long as there is a password. That's enough for me... it does not bother me where the results go, as long as my doctor knows about my condition and my health every day...

4.4.3.2 Lack of Physical Presence of a Health Care Provider

The next concern was "lack of physical presence of a health care provider" (ST10). Participants emphasised that the physical presence of their health care provider and face-to-face visits were essential for them (CA27). One said:

... there is something missing when you use the system because it is sometimes good [to see the doctor]...I think face-to-face communication with your doctor will solve many other problems, it is not only the examination of your heart, lungs or blood pressure. Communication is important for me....

While emphasising the importance of receiving the benefits of face-to-face visits with the medical doctor (a health care provider) from time to time, most patients stated that they would prefer to take their measurements themselves and visit their medical doctor only when something additional to the services achievable by the HTMS were required. For example:

It would be better to see the doctor or nurse at home, but it shouldn't only be to measure our blood pressure reading. It should be something more important than that to drag a doctor here. We like our doctors but we don't want to see them too often…If you think it is necessary for you to visit your family doctor, then you should visit him. Nothing should stop you from seeing your doctors.

4.4.3.3 Equipment Reliability

Several participants were concerned about the reliability of equipment (CA28), for example:

… When the system is down, how are we going to find out about our condition? A machine is a machine. Sometimes, the machine goes wrong. It's difficult to trust a machine.

Several participants pointed to past experiences with medical instruments to take routine measurements (such as blood pressure devices), which had been inaccurate. They were interested to know to what extent the system was reliable and what processes had been implemented to recognise wrong measurements. One said:

I bought an electronic blood pressure monitor about two years ago, after 2–3 months I realised that the blood pressure measurements were different compared to what the doctor was taking and I did not use it anymore. I like to know how reliable the system is. If the measurement was not correct, how would we know?

4.4.3.4 Concern about HTMS Support

Given that most medical doctors are very busy, some participants expressed concerns about whether medical doctors would support such a system (CA29). For example:

… What about the practitioner, because he has to spend extra time to look at it… if the doctor has 20 patients in a queue and she spends about 10 min with each patient, I don't think she will have the time to deal with this system.

Some participants were concerned about technical support and maintaining the system (CA30), for example:

As is true for all machines, like cars or whatever, I think this system needs to be regularly maintained to make sure it works properly or if it needs repair… who is responsible for that?

4.4.3.5 Cost

Participants were concerned about the cost of providing an HTMS and maintenance expenses associated with technical and clinical support (CA31). This was exemplified by one participant's observation:

I would use it, but I suppose a lot of other people, would be reluctant to use this system due to the costs of this and the installation, obviously, it's going to be pretty expensive... I only worry about the price whether I can afford to buy this system.

4.4.3.6 Training Programs for Patients who are Going to Use the HTMS

Participants generally agreed that particular attention should be paid to designing an appropriate training program (CA32) for the HTMS, for example:

...Training is important, particularly in older people like myself... the person who needs to use the system should be sat down by an expert and told exactly what to do step by step... The information has to be repeated until we learn and given practice on using the system until we can properly manage it on our own. The training is very important in our age. As for you guys it is easy, but for us it's not.

4.4.4 The Impact on Health Care Services

4.4.4.1 Impact on Access to Health Care

Most participants thought the HTMS would improve access to healthcare, particularly for elderly homebound patients with chronic disease (CA34) and those who live in remote areas (CA35). For example:

I cannot speak English. I have no legs, and I have had an operation on my heart, I can't move at all, I can barely go to the bathroom... this system is very helpful for people that are homebound, I think it's a great idea for people who can't get out of their home.

Several participants also said the system would improve access to medical services even in metropolitan areas (CA36), for example:

It is not only helpful for rural areas even in the cities like in Sydney and other metropolitan areas, it is really hard to ring up a doctor and get them to come and see you...

4.4.4.2 The Impact on Use of Health Care Services

The majority of patients agreed that the HTMS could reduce the number of emergency department visits and hospital admissions (CA37). To support this claim they referred to the preventative role of the HTMS in providing an early warning of health status deterioration. For example, one participant argued:

...if you use the system regularly, it is possible to know the problem at the very beginning. You can go to see a doctor and avoid emergency.

Likewise, they believed that the HTMS could reduce the number of medical practitioner visits (CA38). For example

...if you use the system at home still you have to visit the doctor, but at least you don't have to go (to the doctor) frequently.

4.4.5 Suggestions

The participants made suggestions to improve patients' acceptance of the system. The most common was the development of a multi-user HTMS rather than the single user version. Another suggestion was developing a multi-language prototype. This could include adding voices, which instruct patients at each stage and provide necessary feedback to them about their health status. Since moving the mouse was problematic for some patients such as those who had Parkinson's disease, several patients suggested supplying the system with a touch screen facility. A final suggestion was the inclusion of normal ranges on measurements, with indications to inform patients when their measurements exceeded the normal limits and to deliver relevant action plans.

4.5 Discussion

Although the design of this study precludes generalisation, it does provide some insights into aspects of the HTMS. Patients' concerns centred on the issues of cost, ease of use, clinical support, low self-efficacy and anxiety related to the use of the HTMS, most participants expressed positive attitudes toward the HTMS and intended to use the system. It is notable that 'attitude' has been considered one of the main determinants of 'intention to use' (Davis 1986).

They mentioned several advantages of the HTMS such as improving access to healthcare services, peace of mind, convenience, empowering patients to participate in their health management, improving patient's health management by physicians, reducing the number of medical and emergency department visits and hospital admissions, which could result in saving time and cost. These are in general agreement with patients' perceptions of home telecare reported by other investigators (Demiris 2000; Agrell et al. 2000; Finkelstein et al. 1999; Mair et al. 2000; Whitten and Collins 1998; Pare et al. 2006).

Although some participants expressed a low level of confidence in using the system, most agreed that the system would be useful and mentioned that they intended to use it. In fact, the findings of this study suggest that 'perceived usefulness' is likely to be an important factor in the acceptance of the HTMS. This is consistent with the TAM of Davis (1989, 1986), which proposed 'perceived usefulness' to be the major determinant of 'intention to use'. Also it was found that users will adopt a new IT system if they perceive the system useful, even if they dislike it (Davis 1989; McFarland and Hamilton 2006), suggesting that patients' should be made aware of the useful aspects of the system in order to improve their acceptance.

Patients' perceptions of 'ease of use' of the system varied widely within and among focus groups. There was a diverse range of statements from extremely easy to extremely difficult to use. Likewise, participants' judgments about their capabilities to use the system varied greatly, suggesting different levels of HTMS self-efficacy among participants.

In this study some participants reported fear of using such a system. There is evidence that 'computer anxiety', which is referred to as a negative psychological reaction to computers (Rosen and Magurie 1990), has a significant negative impact on attitude (Igbaria and Chakrabarti 1990; Parasuraman and Igbaria 1990), 'intention' (Elasmar and Carter 1996), 'behaviour' (McFarland and Hamilton 2006; Compeau and Higgins 1995; Todman and Monaghan 1994) and 'performance' (Anderson 1996; Heinssen et al. 1987). Also there is evidence that 'computer anxiety' is negatively related to 'computer self-efficacy' (Igbaria and Chakrabarti 1990; Compeau and Higgins 1995; Heinssen et al. 1987; Wilfong 2006).

Numerous studies have used an enhanced version of TAM, depending on the context of the studies (McFarland and Hamilton 2006; Karahanna and Straub 1999; Dishaw and Strong 1999; Igbaria et al. 1997; Venkatesh and Davis 1996; Taylor and Todd 1995). Davis et al. (1989) indicated that computer anxiety and computer selfefficacy affect PEOU. The findings of Venkatesh and Davis (1996) have also supported self-efficacy as a determinant of PEOU. Jay (1981), Rosen and Maguire (1990) conceptualised computer anxiety as an affective factor related to technophobia, associated with the degree of computer usage. Hu et al. (1999) used the TAM in the context of telemedicine technology to study physicians' acceptance. Since relatively low variance was explained by the TAM in that particular context, they suggested that the augmentation of the TAM with additional measures such as self-efficacy might improve its explanatory power in that context. The findings of this study suggest that in order to develop training for patients to use HTMS, it is likely to be helpful to tailor training components to reduce 'HTMS anxiety' and improve 'HTMS self-efficacy'. Many studies (Torkzadeh and Koufteros 1994; Sadri and Robertson 1993; Briggs 1988) have indicated that training could improve computer self-efficacy.

Although patients were informed that they did not need any computer knowledge to use the HTMS and it is not a PC, some still viewed the system as a computer. The practical implication is that in any HTMS introductory presentation or training programs, it should be emphasised strongly that there is no requirement to have any knowledge about computers and it is suggested the HTMS is designed so that it does not look like a PC.

A few participants mentioned the HTMS would not be useful for people who live near health care services. However most participants believed the system would improve access to health care services, particularly for those who live in remote areas (e.g. rural areas and r mote suburbs in metropolitan areas). Participants agreed that being aware of their health conditions and the ability to have their health conditions regularly monitored could give them peace of mind and reduce the feeling of isolation.

Participants agreed that the HTMS would save cost and time by reducing hospital admissions, emergency department and medical practitioner visits and associated travel. However, they mentioned that it was difficult at this stage to be definitive about the issue of cost until more information was available regarding the cost of the HTMS and its maintenance.

The findings of this study suggest that cost would be one of the most important factors related to the intention to use the HTMS. Since most target users are elderly people, often with limited incomes, the practical implication is the HTMS would need to be provided at affordable prices.

Therefore, before the marketing phase, conducting a careful study of the average income of the target population is recommended. In addition, support by the government or health insurance companies to overcome the problem of cost is likely to promote the diffusion of HTMS technology.

Although several participants believed it would save medical doctors' time by providing easy access to accurate updated information about the patients' health condition, most were concerned about adequate clinical support by medical practitioners. In fact, affordability and physicians' acceptance were among the main concerns. Therefore, physicians' acceptance of the HTMS needs to be investigated.

Participants agreed that the HTMS could inform patients of their health conditions, thus promoting active participation in their health management and empowering them to perform better self-care, by providing easy access to useful information about their diseases and up-to-date information about their health conditions. Several participants also pointed out that the HTMS could improve their compliance with medication and treatment, which could affect clinical outcomes. Also, participants agreed that the HTMS could improve the health management by the latter physicians by providing more accurate and up-to-date information, which might help to make better decisions. Participants agreed that the HTMS could play a preventative role in terms of providing early warning when their health conditions were deteriorating, which could lead to on-time appropriate intervention. The latter may reduce the use of emergency services and hospital admissions.

Although a few participants were concerned about confidentiality of the information and believed that sending the data through the Internet was not secure, most of them were not concerned about confidentiality of data and the transfer of information via the Internet.

This was as long as there was password protection and standard data security measures in place.

Most participants preferred to use the system and take their measurements on their own rather than receiving home visits to provide such services (services, which are achievable by HTMS). However, they believed that they needed the physical presence of a health care provider to enjoy face-to-face visits from time to time, when there was something more important to be performed than what was achievable by the HTMS. It seems patients' preferences for taking their measurements themselves may be related to their desire to participate in their health management as well as the associated difficulties of getting medical doctors to visit

Table 4.4 Implications of the findings of this study with respect to theoretical framework, development and implementation

Findings	Implications
In relation to theoretical framework of patients' acceptance of HTMS	It is proposed that the two constructs, HTMS self-efficacy and anxiety be included in future HTMS acceptance models
Patients' concerns related to cost	HTMS needs to be provided at affordable prices. Therefore, before the marketing phase, conducting careful study of the average income of the target population is recommended. In addition, support by the government or health insurance companies to overcome the problem of cost is likely to promote the diffusion of HTMS technology
Patients' concerns related to "ease of use", HTMS self-efficacy and anxiety	Not only does the HTMS need to be as easy as possible to use, the tailored program needs to be developed to be able to be customised according to individuals' levels of HTMS self-efficacy and anxiety to improve their HTMS self-efficacy and decrease HTMS anxiety
Some patients perceived the system as a computer, despite being informed they did not need any computer knowledge to use the HTMS, and it is not a PC	In any HTMS introductory presentation or training programs, it should be emphasised strongly that there is no requirement to have any knowledge about computers and it is suggested the HTMS is designed so that it does not look like a PC
Patients' concerns related to adequate clinical support of HTMS by physicians	Physicians' acceptance of the HTMS needs to be investigated and promoted before implementation of major HTMS initiatives
Patients' perceptions of HTMS were generally positive	Consistent with patients' perceptions of home telecare reported by other investigators
Patients suggested practical implications	• Development of a multi-user HTMS rather than the single user version • Development of a multi-language prototype. • Addition of voices, which instruct patients at each stage • Provision of necessary feedback to the patients about their health status • Modification of the system with a touch screen facility for those with tremors • Inclusion of normal ranges on measurements, with indications to inform patients when their measurements exceeded the normal limits and which deliver relevant action plans

their homes to provide services which are achievable by the HTMS. Patients' usage of the HTMS should not deprive them of gaining psychological benefits which can be obtained by the physical presence and face-to-face visits of a health care provider from time to time.

While the TAM (Davis 1989; 1986) was found to be an effective model, there are clearly other meaningful factors. In this regards, Davis (1993) proposed that additional factors should be added to the TAM (based on the study contexts). The findings of this study suggested 'HTMS self-efficacy' and 'HTMS (or in general, modern technology) anxiety' (Rahimpour 2006) are likely to be important in the acceptance of HTMS by the target population. Therefore, it is proposed that these two factors be incorporated in developing a model for patients' acceptance of HTMS. Implications of the findings of this study with respect to theoretical framework, development and implementation have been summarised in Table 4.4.

4.6 Conclusions

In this study, participants were recruited from different ethnic backgrounds to include the main ethnic groups in the south east area of Sydney. However, an important limitation is that the possible impact of cultural factors on patients' perceptions and acceptance of HTMS was not studied. Cultural factors may affect some aspects of patients' perceptions of HTMS. Therefore, it is suggested that in the future there would be merit in conducting a study of the impact of cultural factors on HTMS acceptance.

> **Summary points**
>
> What is already known on the topic?
>
> - Earlier researchers suggested that there has been a paucity of robust qualitative studies of home telecare.
> - To the best of our knowledge, previous qualitative studies of patients' acceptance of home telecare have not been based on established technology acceptance theories.
>
> What this study added to our knowledge?
>
> - Whilst the findings of this study were generally consistent with previous home telecare studies, this is the first study to identify HTMS anxiety and self-efficacy as important variables that should be included in future HTMS acceptance models
> - This study informs the development of the HTMS acceptance model which is the theoretical framework for the next stage of our research.

Although self-efficacy and anxiety are constructs that have been included in research on people's use of technology, they have not been used in any previous study of home telecare, where technical innovation is applied to managing chronic healthcare in elderly patients unaccustomed to modern technology.

The findings of this study suggest that HTMS self-efficacy and anxiety are likely to be important constructs in patients' acceptance of home telecare. Therefore, we propose these two factors be included in future HTMS acceptance models.

The consistent responses from this sample across a wide range of ethnic groups, lays a number of important foundations in terms of the design and implementation of HTMS. They help us to understand the drivers of acceptance in order to proactively design interventions (e.g., tailoring user training programs to address issues such as HTMS anxiety and HTMS selfefficacy) targeting patients who less readily adopt HTMS than others, and consequently, maximise the patients' acceptance of the technology and promote its effective diffusion.

Acknowledgments

Competing interests

BC and NL declare that they are directors of MedCare Systems Pty. Ltd. (Sydney, NSW, Australia) which supplied the pre-production prototype of the Home Telecare Management System used in the evaluation.

Authors' contribution

MR performed the data collection and substantive data analysis. JM, NL, and BC contributed to the trial design, data analysis and drafting and review of the manuscript.

References

Abrams, D. J., & Geier, M. R. (2006). A comparison of patient satisfaction with telehealth and on-site consultations: A pilot study for prenatal genetic counselling. *Journal of Genetic Counseling, 15*(3), 199–205.

Agrell, H., Dahlberg, S., & Jerant, A. F. (2000). Patients' perceptions regarding home telecare. *Telemedicine and E Health Journal, 6*(4), 409–415.

Anderson, A. (1996). Predictors of computer anxiety and performance in information systems. *Computers in Human Behavior, 12*(1), 61–77.

Bandura, A. (1997). *Self-efficacy: The exercise of control.* New York: W.H. Freeman and Company.

Briggs, P. (1988). What we know and what we need to know: The user model versus the user's model in human-computer interaction. *Behaviour Information Technology, 7*(4), 431–442.

Brignell, M., Wootton, R., & Gray, L., (2007). The application of telemedicine to geriatric medicine, age and ageing, doi:10.1093/ageing/afm045, published online on April 20, 2007.

Celler, B. G., Lovell, N. H., & Basilakis, J. (2003). Using information technology to improve the management of chronic disease. *Medical Journal of Australia, 179*(5), 242–246.

Chae, Y. M., Heon Lee, J., Hee Ho, S., Ja Kim, H., Hong Jun, K., & Uk Won, J. (2001). Patient satisfaction with telemedicine in home health services for the elderly. *International Journal of Medical Informatics, 61*(2–3), 167–173.

Chang, M. K. (1998). Predicting unethical behavior: A comparison of the theory of reasoned action and the theory of planned behavior. *Journal of Business Ethics, 17*(16), 1825–1834.

Chumbler, N. R., Mann, W. C., Wu, S., Schmid, A., & Kobb, R. (2004). The association of home-cognitive functioning frail elderly men. *Telemedicine and E Health Journal, 10*(2), 129–137.

Compeau, D. R., & Higgins, C. A. (1995). Application of social cognitive theory to training for computer skills. *Information System Research, 6*(2), 118–143.

Davis, F., (1986). A technology acceptance model for empirically testing new end-user information system: Theory and results, Doctorate Dissertation, Sloan School of Management, MIT, 1986

Davis, F. (1989). Perceived usefulness, perceived ease of use, and user acceptance of information technology. *MIS Quarterly, 13*(3), 319–339.

Davis, F. (1993). User acceptance of information technology: System characteristics, user perceptions and behavioral impacts. *International Journal for Man-Machine Studies, 38*, 475–487.

Davis, F., Bagozzi, R., & Warshaw, P. (1989). User acceptance of computer technology: A comparison of two theoretical models. *Management Science, 35*(8), 982–1003.

Demiris, G. (2000). *Patients' perception and interaction in a home care based telemedicine project*, Doctorate Dissertation, Graduate School of the University of Minnesota, Minnesota.

Demiris, G., Rantz, M. J., Aud, M. A., Marek, K. D., Tyrer, H. W., Skubic, M., et al. (2004). Older adults' attitudes towards and perceptions of smart home technologies: A pilot study. *Medical Informatics and the Internet in Medicine, 29*(2), 87–94.

Demiris, G., Speedie, S., & Finkelstein, S. (2000). A questionnaire for the assessment of patients' impressions of the risks and benefits of home telecare. *Journal of Telemedicine and Telecare, 6*(5), 278–284.

Demiris, G., Speedie, S. M., & Finkelstein, S. (2001). Change of patients' perceptions of telehomecare. *Telemedicine Journal and E Health, 7*(3), 241–248.

Dick, P. T., Filler, R., & Pavan, A. (1999). Participant satisfaction and comfort with multi disciplinary pediatric telemedicine consultations. *Journal of Pediatric Surgery, 34*(1), 137–141.

Dishaw, M. T., & Strong, D. M. (1999). Extending the technology acceptance model with task-technology fit constructs. *Information and Management, 36*(1), 9–21.

Elasmar, M. G., & Carter, M. E. (1996). Use of e-mail by college-students and implications for curriculum. *Journalism & Mass Communication Educator, 51*(2), 46–54.

Finkelstein, S., Speedie, S., Demiris, G., Veen, M., Lundgren, J. M., & Potthoff, S. (2004). Telehomecare: quality, perception, satisfaction. *Telemedicine Journal and E Health, 10*(2), 122–128.

Finkelstein, S., Speedie, S., Hoff, M., & Demeris, G. (1999). Tele-homecare: Telemedicine in home health care. In: *Proceedings/IEEE Engineering in Medicine and Biology Society* (vol. 21, p. 681). Monash University, Caulfield.

Fishbein, M., & Ajzen, I. (1975). *Belief, attitude intention and behavior: An introduction to theory and research*. Reading: Addison-Wesley.

Fontana, A., & Frey, J. H. (1994). Interviewing. In N. K. Denzin & Y. S. Lincoln (Eds.), *Handbook of qualitative research* (pp. 361–374). Thousand Oaks: Sage.

Heinssen, R. K., Glass, C. R., & Knight, L. A. (1987). Assessing computer anxiety: Development and validation of the computer anxiety rating scale. *Computers in Human Behavior, 3*, 49–59.

Hu, P. J., Chau, P. Y. K., Liu Sheng, O. R., & Kar Yan, T. (1999). Examining the technology acceptance model using physician acceptance of telemedicine technology. *Journal of Management Information Systems, 16*(2), 91–112.

Igbaria, M. (1993). User acceptance of microcomputer technology: An empirical test. *OMEGA The International Journal of Management Science, 21*(1), 73–90.

Igbaria, M., & Chakrabarti, A. (1990). Computer anxiety and attitudes towards microcomputer use. *Behaviour and Information Technology, 9*(3), 229–241.

Igbaria, M., Zinatelli, N., Cragg, P., & Cavaya, A. L. M. (1997). Personal computing acceptance factors in small firms: A structural equation model. *MIS Quarterly, 21*(3), 279–302.

Jay, T. (1981). Computerphobia: What to do about it. *Educational Technology, 21*, 47–48.

Karahanna, E., & Straub, D. W. (1999). The psychological origins of perceived usefulness and ease-of-use. *Information and Management, 35*(4), 237–250.

King, W., & Jun, H. (2006). A meta-analysis of the technology acceptance model. *Information and Management, 43*(6), 740–755.

Liu, X., Sawada, Y., Takizawa, T., Sato, H., Sato, M., & Sakamoto, H., et al. (2007). Doctor-patient communication: A comparison between telemedicine consultation and face-to-face consultation. *Internal Medicine, 46*(5), 227–232.

Lovell, N. H., Celler, B. G., Basilakis, J., Magrabi, F., Huynh, K., & Mathie, M. (2002). Managing chronic disease with home telecare: A system architecture and case study. *EMBS/BMES Conference, 3,* 1896–1897.

Mair, F., Whitten, P., May, C., & Doolittle, G. C. (2000). Patients' perceptions of a telemedicine specialty clinic. *Journal of Telemedicine and Telecare, 6*(1), 36–40.

McFarland, D., & Hamilton, D. (2006). Adding contextual specificity to the technology acceptance model. *Computers in Human Behavior, 22*(3), 427–447.

Mekhjian, H., Turner, J. W., Gailiun, M., & McCain, T. A. (1999). Patient satisfaction with telemedicine in a prison environment. *Journal of Telemedicine and Telecare, 5*(1), 55–61.

Palmas, W., Teresi, J., Morin, P., Wolff, L. T., Field, L., Eimicke, J. P., et al. (2006). Recruitment and enrolment of rural and urban medically underserved elderly into a randomized trial of telemedicine case management for diabetes care. *Telemedicine Journal and E. Health, 12*(5), 601–607.

Parasuraman, S., & Igbaria, M. (1990). An examination of gender differences in the determinants of computer anxiety and attitudes toward microcomputers among managers. *International Journal of Man-Machine Studies, 32*(3), 327–340.

Pare, G., Sicotte, C., St-Jules, D., & Gauthier, R. (2006). Cost-minimization analysis of a telehomecare program for patients with chronic obstructive pulmonary disease. *Telemedicine Journal and E Health, 12*(2), 114–121.

Rahimpour, M. (2006) *Developing a model for patients' acceptance of home telecare.* Master dissertation, Graduate School of Biomedical Engineering, University of New South Wales, Australia.

Ritchie, J. (2001). Not everything can be reduced to numbers. In C. Bergland (Ed.), *Health research* (pp. 150–173). Melbourne: Oxford University Press.

Rosen, L., & Magurie, P. (1990). Myths and realities of computerphobia: A meta-analysis. *Anxiety Research, 3,* 175–191.

Sadri, G., & Robertson, I. (1993). Self-Efficacy, Work-related behavior: A review and meta-analysis. *Applied Psychology: An International Review, 42*(2), 139–152.

Szajna, B. (1996). Empirical evaluation of the revised technology acceptance model. *Management Science, 42*(1), 85–92.

Taylor, S., & Todd, P. (1995). Assessing IT usage: The role of prior experience. *MIS Quarterly, 19*(4), 561–570.

Todman, J., & Monaghan, E. (1994). Qualitative differences in computer experience, computer anxiety, and students' use of computers: A path model. *Computers in Human Behavior, 10*(4), 529–539.

Torkzadeh, G., & Koufteros, X. (1994). Factorial validity of a computer self-efficacy scale and the impact of computer training. *Educational and Psychological Measurement, 54*(3), 813–821.

Venkatesh, V., & Davis, F. D. (1996). A model of the antecedents of perceived ease of use: Development and test. *Decision Sciences, 27*(3), 451–481.

Whitten, P., & Collins, B. (1998). Nurse reactions to a prototype home telemedicine system. *Journal of Telemedicine and Telecare, 4*(Suppl. 1), 50–52.

Whitten, P., Mair, F., & Collins, B. (1997). Home telenursing in Kansas: Patients' perceptions of uses and benefits. *Journal of Telemedicine and Telecare, 3*(Suppl. 1), 67–69.

Wilfong, J. (2006). Computer anxiety and anger: The impact of computer use, computer experience and self-efficacy beliefs. *Computers in Human Behavior, 22*(6), 1001–1011.

Woods, K. F., Kutlar, A., Johnson, J. A., Waller, J. L., Grigsby, R. K., Stachura, M. E., et al. (1999). Sickle cell telemedicine and standard clinical encounters: A comparison of patient satisfaction. *Telemedicine Journal, 5*(4), 349–356.

Chapter 5
A Framework for Future Studies of Personalised Medicine: Affordance, Travelling, and Governance of Expertise

Morten Sager, Fredrik Bragesjö and Aant Elzinga

Abstract Through individualised genomic knowledge and the digital tools of telemedicine, personalised treatments may be able to solve the "irresolvable" conflict between the evidence-based and person-centred medicine movements. The aim of this chapter is to offer a framework for future work concerning these developments. As indispensable human elements are often rendered invisible with these technologies, expertise is critical. Furthermore, it is important to consider the unpredictable and transformative effects of materialities and, consequently, how expertise travels. The pursuit of analytical work without acceptance of the general and often abstract polarisation between evidence and persons in internal medical debates requires acknowledgement of both the distribution of expertise and influence (e.g., the governance of expertise). Finally, hybrids of humans and non-humans are ubiquitous but require scrutiny. That is, the affordance of technologies that embody, enclose and translate expertise in new forms has reconfiguring effects on the roles of experts and physician-patient relationships.

Keywords Evidence-based medicine • Personalised medicine • Affordance • Governance • Expertise • Telemedicine

5.1 Introduction

Prophecies made in high-impact journals identify personalised medicine—or predictive, preventive and personalised medicine (PPPM)—as the goal for global health.[1] Through the systematic combination of genomic, proteomic and digital communication

---

[1] The more generic and all-embracing term is likely personalis(z)ed medicine; see, for example, Singer 2010; Bourret 2005; Hedgecoe 2006; Hedgecoe and Martin 2003; Mezzich et al. 2011; Paci and Ibarreta 2009. For reasons of brevity and to provide a contrast to the concept of person-centred medicine, we frequently use the abbreviated form PPPM.

M. Sager (✉) · F. Bragesjö · A. Elzinga
University of Gothenburg, Gothenburg, Sweden
e-mail: morten.sager@gu.se

K. Wasen (ed.), *Emerging Health Technology*, SpringerBriefs in Health Care Management and Economics, DOI: 10.1007/978-3-642-32570-0_5, © The Author(s) 2013

technologies, the idea of personalised medicine involves the mapping of an individual's health risk profile and the prevention of disease onset with high precision.

One reason for PPPM's appeal is its reconciliation of two often contradicting concerns evident in two other major health trends: the quest for more scientific facts in evidence-based medicine (EBM) and the focus on patients and personal skills in person-centred care (Bohlin and Sager 2011; Bird 2011; Croft et al. 2011; Holmes et al. 2006; Torpy et al. 2009). PPPM lays claim to the area between the epidemiological subpopulations of EBM and the individual patients of person-centred care by drawing on the intensive use of information and communication technology (ICT), such as the internet, and new systematic genomic and proteomic knowledge gained from global mapping efforts (Golubnitschaja 2010; Collins et al. 2006). PPPM integrates an entire complex of emerging technologies that propel transformations at multiple levels. Some experts view these technologies, which include telemedicine, e-health and e-care, as positively influencing the social environments of patients and enhancing methods of (self-)monitoring.[2] Some prominent Science and Technology Studies (STS) scholars also have this view.[3] Pharmoeconomics is another field in which patient adherence is studied and provides knowledge that supports arguments for the reduction of the costs that non-adherence incurs both for the patient and society (cf. the journal PharmacoEconomics). There is a rapidly growing market of new and emerging diagnostic instruments with origins in pharmacogenetics, which is the science that seeks to determine how people's genetic composition affects their responses to

---

[2] The concept of telemedicine is not easily defined: see, for example, Oudshoorn 2012. Sood et al. (2007) reviews one hundred different definitions that have been proposed since the 1970s and that range from surgical robotics to emails. Some authors have suggested that the concept of telemedicine should be replaced by (or at least incorporated into) the notion of e-health, partly due to the many failures of what we often associate with the traditional initiatives of telemedicine. However, as Petersson 2011, p. 86), writes, "[e]ven though telemedicine seems to live a dangerous life, this should by no means be interpreted as the abolishing of the dream to improve healthcare by the use of distance bridging technology. There is an endless stream of technologies brought forward to accomplish increased quality of care by rationalization through ICT, but they go, today, under other names and are framed somewhat differently such as telecare, taking these ICT's outside of the hospital into people's homes and out of the territory of medicine into the turf of care, the use of the general concept of IT to involve also administration and management, and e-health (rarely called a technology) to point to the need to prevent people from abusing healthcare resources by making sure they live a healthy life and keep themselves updated on their health on-line". The notion of e-health is defined even more broadly than telemedicine and is associated with electronic health records, consumer health informatics, health knowledge management and healthcare information systems, as well as traditional telemedicine. In a review that identifies 51 unique definitions of e-health, Oh et al. 2005 refer to the work of Ludwig Wittgenstein and suggest that there is a rather clear understanding of what e-health is but that it is difficult or even impossible to provide a proper definition in words. An overview of an entire range of self-management tools, a typology of differing device complexities and a discussion of four forces that influence the rapid development of a new market (clinical care, economics and politics, consumerism, and technological innovation) is found in Barrett 2005.

[3] For support of this view, see, e.g., May et al. 2003; Oudshoorn 2011, 2012. For reviews of the field of STS, see Hackett et al. 2007; Sismondo 2004; Yearley 2005.

medicines and which offers the potential to develop a new generation of medicines that are tailored to individual needs. In addition, it is hoped that genomically based diagnostic tests will deliver reliable and rapid diagnostic data to healthcare professionals in the future (Royal Society 2005). Although pharmacogenetics has thus far had little influence on clinical practice, visions of rapid advances in both the science and the underpinning of genetic technologies strongly influence research programs, including those in Europe, where the EU's Directorate General for Science and Innovation is a major actor in the promotion of S&T for relevant genomics, proteomics and other "-omics" developments.[4]

Historically, high-tech solutions have created hype and the associated unconditional acceptance, or, in contrast, great fear, cf. gene therapy (Grankvist 2011) or stem cells (Sager 2006), none of which appear to contribute to an enhanced realisation of the desired health benefits. Because of the grand visions and rapid development in this context, the interplay of these emerging e-health technologies vis-à-vis human expertise necessitates an empirical analysis of the reconfigurations of the healthcare system.[5] How will these developments affect the physician-patient relationship and how will physician's and patient's identities affect the roles of emerging technologies and medical and lay expertise?

Long-standing conversations on knowledge and expertise, such as those occurring within STS, have addressed emerging health technologies (Oudshoorn 2011; Brown and Webster 2004; Cartwright 2000; Clarke et al. 2003; Webster 2006;

---

[4] See, for example, the EC workshop in Brussels 2011-05-13/14 on European Perspectives on Personalised Medicine: http://ec.europa.eu/research/health/events-06_en.html; the EC workshop on Biomarkers for Patient Stratification—2010-06-10/11, http://ec.europa.eu/research/health/pdf/biomarkers-for-patient-stratification_en.pdf; and the earlier workshop on "omics" in Personalised Medicine—2010-05-29/30, http://ec.europa.eu/research/health/pdf/summary-report-omics-for-personalised-medicine-workshop_en.pdf.

[5] The notion of expertise has a long history within STS and has been discussed in various ways. For human's expertise in relation to artificial intelligence (AI), see Collins and Kusch 1998. This discussion has clear connections to the dispute between pure sociological accounts for explaining the production of scientific knowledge and accounts that leave analytical space for the agency of materiality and technology so that the technoscientific process can be understood. For a review and an attempt to resolve the dispute with a specific definition of the concept of *co-production*, see Jasanoff 2004; see also Bloor 1999a; Bloor 1999b; Callon and Latour 1992; Collins and Yearley 1992a, b; Pickering 1992; Woolgar 1992. However, this discussion should not be confused with the more philosophical discussion of AI, for which John Searle's (Searle 1980) Chinese example is a common reference. For philosophical accounts of AI, also see Boden 1996; Cole 2009; Searle 1999; Dreyfus et al. 1986. One other aspect of the notion of expertise relates more to the role of STS and the relation to their objects of study. The debate commenced after Collins and Evans 2002, argued that when studying an area of research, the researchers within STS acquire different forms of expertise: The more we study an issue or field, the more knowledge we gain about it. In addition, they presented a method for measuring expertise, including the expertise both of researchers within a field and of the researcher studying that very field. Furthermore, it was suggested that the expertise of STSers could be of importance for the objects of study or for the politicians who address the uncertain knowledge claims of various experts. By using this framework, it would be possible to determine who is a proper expert and who is not. Collins and a few associates have continued this research: Collins 2004, 2007, 2009, Evans and Collins 2007; Collins and Evans 2007; Selinger and Crease 2006.

Hindmarsh and Prainsack 2010; Salter et al. 2009). A common trait of these studies is a focus on mundane practices in close relation to political and economic infrastructures and the ramifications for the interplay between experts and patients.

Our aim is to develop a three-layered framework for the empirical study of emerging health technologies as illustrated through the example of PPPM and, in particular, telemedicine/e-health technologies. We identify three aspects of research on PPPM that we believe to be especially to both being pursued and combined. The first aspect is the governance of expertise. The last few years has witnessed an abundance of pertinent research in this area. A focus on the governance that is implicated in new distributions of expertise[6] resulting from the mediations of emerging technologies is a vital part of any analysis of PPPM (Hedgecoe 2006; Kerr et al. 2007; Milewa 2006; Oudshoorn 2011, 2012; Weimer 2010). The second aspect is the travelling of expertise. How is the notion of expertise affected by these changes, and where is this expertise located and allocated in the new interfaces among physician, patient and e-health solutions? The final aspect is how different forms of expertise invite multiple uses, that is, their affordance.[7] The notion of affordance is commonly used in contemporary research in various ways (Bergen et al. 2010; Bloomfield et al. 2010; Leonardi 2011), but in early research, Norman (1988) defined affordance as a perceived property of an artefact that suggests how it should be used. A few years later, Pfaffenberger (1992, p. 284) adds that "Affordances are inherently multiple: Differing perceptions lead to different uses. You can drink water from a cup to quench thirst, but you can also use a cup to show you are well bred, to emphasise your taste in choosing decor, or to hold framework airplane parts". However, this multiplicity is not unconstrained: you cannot use the cup for intercontinental travels.[8]

If we combine affordance with governance, we can observe how various material cultures are utilised when expertise travels. Different materialities offer different sets of possibilities and limitations. Technological devices or genetic microarrays could be used to enhance the interaction between the healthcare system and patients, or guidelines, protocols, algorithms or even organisational forms, such as formal or informal networks, should perhaps conduct these duties. Different materialities enable, or afford, rather than determine, different

---

[6] For studies on the relationship between expertise and governance, see Chamberlain 2010, 2011; Corburn 2007; Cornwall and Shankland 2008; Ford-Eickhoff et al. 2011; Lofgren and de Boer 2004; Marcant 2008; Moore 2010; Runhaar et al. 2009; Wilkinson et al. 2010; Stephanie 2010.

[7] Concerning the focus on affordance in the threefold framework we owe great thanks to Mats Fridlund at the Department of Philosophy, Linguistics and Theory of Science, University of Gothenburg, who was instrumental in bringing the notion to the centre of our attention.

[8] In these early discussions of affordance, scholars use examples of artefacts and technologies to make their argument; we want to stress that affordance should not be understood only in these terms. When we use the notion of technology vis-à-vis affordance and expertise, the point of departure is a more contemporary meaning of the concept found in STS; here, it is often used in the context of sociotechnical ensembles in which the stability, materiality, hardness or even existence of technologies are more or less open-ended (see, e.g., Latour 1999). Also see Gibson 1979, p. 129.

relationships between actors in healthcare systems. For example, patients may be empowered and/or disempowered, or the autonomy of doctors may be confirmed and/or constrained in various new ways (Mort et al. 2009).

First, we will map key concepts, problems and areas of research in new and emerging technologies, including PPPM, telemedicine, e-health and e-care, and lastly, pharmacogenomics. Second, the developments of and the tensions between EBM and person-centred medicine, as a replacement for traditional patient-centred medicine, will be described. Against this background, we will then suggest a future mode of analysis for these considerable reconfigurations of the healthcare system. The combined concepts of the governance of expertise, travelling expertise and the affordance of technologies are presented as a helpful analytical lens for highlighting essential aspects of these developments and are employed in an illustrative case study. As will be demonstrated, the framework will enable a detailed focus on the dynamic relationships between expertise and materiality.

5.2 Powerful, Predictive, Preventive and Personalised Medicine

Leroy Hood, the inventor of the first automated DNA sequencing machine, claims that "personalized medicine is too narrow a view of what is coming" (Singer 2010). Singer states that the shift will be much broader and will involve a move from reactive medicine to proactive medicine. According to Hood, medical practice of the future is characterised by four P's: **p**owerfully **p**redictive, **p**ersonalised and **p**reventive, with a focus on wellness and patient participation. Hood identifies the following technologies as important in this context:

- Digital technology, for storing and managing medical records with genetic information (this practice will also require suitable security systems so that personal integrity will be ensured).
- Nanotechnology, for measuring 2,500 proteins in a single drop of blood, a practice whose use is increasing [for information on the hopes and risks related to nanomedicine, see (European Commission 2007)].
- Technology, for diagnosing and analysing a single cell so that physicians can be immediately informed of normal mechanisms and disease mechanisms in the body.
- Computational tools.

If these expectations of Hood and other scholars are ever realised, they promise to dilute the traditional healthcare role of physicians in that nurse practitioners will assume functions that were previously performed exclusively by physicians (Royal Society 2005). Thus, there will be a sociological shift in the role that was previously dominated by physicians and that provided them with some of their authority; a new class of professionals, who undertake an increasing number of responsibilities as the new and emerging medical technologies appear online, is emerging. These new professionals may be expected to rely on technology rather than years of education and experience to diagnose and treat patients.

A critical question with regard to these developments asks whose expertise is embodied, strengthened and shifted during the redistribution of influence and the transformation of professional roles.

In addition, according to the Royal Society report, all traditional categories of professionals (doctors, nurses and pharmacists) will clearly require much stronger training in the fundamentals of human genetics so that these professionals can offer and interpret key diagnostic tests. Therefore, traditional tacit knowledge and skills will be partially replaced by new forms of tacit knowledge that are associated with genomic literacy and molecularly based disease classification systems. Furthermore, given the pursuit of more rapid and appropriate means of treatment afforded by advances in pharmacogenetics and new diagnostic methods, what expectations and values are typically associated with or projected onto this powerful technoscientific imagery (Hedgecoe and Martin 2003; Hedgecoe 2006)? Moreover, who ultimately establishes "the conventions that underlie practices, which define the criteria that turn tools and novel entities into operational components of clinical settings" (Bourret 2005, p. 41)? We suggest that the approaches to these issues require a focus on the governance that is implicated in new distributions of expertise resulting from the mediation of emerging technologies.

Multi-level transformations of PPPM (or the 4 Ps, in Hood's terms) are visible in two paradigmatic technologies: telemedicine and pharmacogenomics. Telemedicine has a long history dating back to the American Space program after the Second World War and the need to monitor astronauts at a distance (Petersson 2011), but during recent decades has been facilitated by the advent of the Internet, mobile telephone systems and consumers' consequent access to health information. An indirectly related technological dimension appears in genetics and biotechnology that spurs novel forms of personalised medicine, which, in turn, exert new demands on detailed information flows between patients and their physicians for both diagnosis and treatment. This trend is also related to the influence of genomics on the prescription drug market, which gives the biotechnology sector a growing share of the pharmaceutical industry as a whole if one considers the largest 25 companies in the world in terms of sales of human prescription drugs and vaccines (Camacho et al. 2009).

5.2.1 Telemedicine, E-Health and E-Care

The work of Carl R. May and colleagues (May et al. 2003) is critical to appreciating the effects of telemedicine and e-health technologies. May utilises a constructivist analysis that is associated with STS and addresses problems related to expert-patient interfaces and patient adherence in e-health systems. He poses the following question: could new technologies provide a new way to bridge the gap between the heterogeneous life-world of patients and the codified world of evidence-based medicine by combining qualitative discretionary knowledge, EBM-generated quantitative knowledge and clinical guidelines based on the latter to manage illness?

When embedded in a person-centred, preventive healthcare system, telemedicine may be viewed as a system that offers flexibility in the patient use or self-surveillance of prescribed health parameters. As a complement to traditional face-to-face encounters with physicians, such methods may—but not necessarily—increase adherence to prescribed medication routines. Flexibility and adherence are not necessarily easily combined. This tension prompts questions regarding how patient expertise may be combined with the telemedical system and what elements of this expertise are relevant in this combination. A large market targets lifestyle-related diseases; self-use toolkits are tailored to monitor vital indicators. Examples of such targeted diseases are asthma, Type 2 diabetes, hypertonia, obesity and secondary hyperlipidaemia or hypercholesterolemia.

May et al. (2006) refer to telemedical activities as a new type of clinical encounter in which non-human actors (technological aids) function as intermediaries in doctor-patient interactions to reduce hospital admissions. These authors note that "much of this field of practice is about shifting medicine and healthcare away from hospitals and back into the local community" (May et al. 2006, p. 1027). This shift prompts new practices of governance, also known as "technogovernance", in which "intermediaries are deployed to discipline and frame the individual subjectivities of both patient and doctor [...] and act to distribute accountabilities". Furthermore, it is argued that the epistemological authority of both the doctor's EBM-supported position and the patient's narratives that now include accounts of technologically generated self-knowledge are enhanced. If such enhancements are attainable, the contradicting assumptions regarding the redistribution of influence as a zero-sum game become extremely interesting. In addition to redistributing roles, new technologies may add new value for all parties, although such a scenario would clearly be contingent upon circumstances in specific places.

If technologies are considered mediators between physicians and patients, a further classification may distinguish ICTs from varieties of pharmaceutical, biotechnology and therapeutic medical devices. These devices may function as mediators between a person who uses them and his or her physician. With self-managing patients, the role of the physician then shifts from deliverer of medical care to supervisor (Willems 2000).

However, whether this development entails additional democratisation because patients experience a greater amount of individualisation and person-centred care remains an unanswered question. In contrast, despite patients' beliefs that their encounters with doctors are more democratic and participatory, could the new methods actually represent an entrenchment of the evidence paradigm in a new form? Evidence becomes inscribed in methods/technologies, and the necessary negotiations that are involved in configuring the technology are black-boxed from view.

Entrenchment might be involved in that the new technology now shapes the self-understanding of patients in parametric terms based on categories that are inscribed in the virtual world and supplied by non-human actors. In his earlier days, Jürgen Habermas might have referred to this phenomenon as a further technification of patients' life-worlds.

At the same time, healthcare communications discourse analysts indicate the existence of a process in the other direction whereby medically literate patients develop their own expertise and colonise the physician's world as they combine professional discourse with lay experiential discourse (Candlin 2000). For their part, physicians employ hybridised modes of speaking by interpolating discourses of patients' life-worlds in their clinical discourses; thus, simple opposition between a patient's life-world and a doctor's medical world is thought to be collapsing. This shift has also been described as a shift from a white-coat model to a model of shared decision making (Camacho et al. 2009).

Thus, systems for patient self-regulation influence the epistemological questions of who may be considered an expert, who may not and why. In some of the literature on user participation in decision making regarding science and technology (sometimes referred to as technoscience), scholars claim that laypersons are experts in their own right when the technoscientific imaginaries (Jasanoff and Kim 2009) that are envisaged have a strong influence on their life conditions. Therein, it is held that the boundary between expert and lay knowledge changes. This view has also been founded on other arguments, such as those based on the role of tacit knowledge. In recent years, this same view, which is linked to discourse on the democratisation of science and technology within STS, has been challenged and countered by Harry Collins and Robert Evans (Collins and Evans 2007: see also note 5).

These authors have introduced a threefold typology of different forms of expertise. Apart from the formal propositional knowledge of a physicist or astronomer, for example, Collins and Evens identify two additional forms of expertise. One of these forms of expertise is known as "contributory expertise", which a person possesses if s/he is fully immersed in the specialist language and specific research culture. In theory, a layperson could consequently contribute to a scientific field without formal training or credentials. It must be emphasised that this scenario is mere theory; the actual occurrence of this scenario is highly unlikely. This implausibility is why Collins has been accused of creating, or reinstating, a new demarcation in science that is scientific in spirit and possibly technocratic in practice (see note 5). However, contributory expertise is distinguished from another form of expertise. "Interactional expertise" refers to instances in which a layperson is immersed in the specialist linguistic culture of a practical domain rather than a practice itself (Collins 2004). This typology has relevant implications for analyses of the tension between evidence-based expertise that is advocated by specialists "in the know" and the personal knowledge of patients who are also "in the know" in their own ways. The previous arguments may also be extended to issues regarding individual self-regulation or the expert (outside) monitoring (with advanced technical devices) of patients. The difference here is parallel to that between an algorithmic or procedural model of expert evidencing and an enculturational model that emphasises contextual contingencies, learning and "intangibles", such as social trust and tacit knowledge (Collins 1992: Postscript).

Thus, the embodiment and transfer of expert knowledge by telemedicine engender several possible ramifications and interpretations that require further analysis: the mutual enhancement of the epistemological authority of both patients and physicians, the technification of the life-worlds of patients, and patient and physician colonisation of one another's "expert repertoires" and worlds.

5.2.2 Pharmacogenomics

Distance and reflexivity are necessary when seeking to understand what Lucy Suchman refers to as the moving interface between the biological and techno-logical (i.e., bodies and machines, respectively) in modern biomedicine. In a recent anthology edited by Johnson and Berner (2010), Suchman reflects on how, through meetings among professionals, patients and their kin, medical practices are restaged as and/or transformed into bodily encounters that are crucially medi-ated and understood through machines (Suchman 2010). This interplay between humans and nonhumans can be found in many layers of pharmacogenomic developments.

Strong economic and political forces, as well as new and emerging technolo-gies, drive the current trend of PPPM. A closely associated vision involves the use of pharmacogenetically based knowledge in diagnostic devices to accelerate patient throughput and tailor medical treatment to individual patient needs at the point-of-care (PoC, i.e., in clinics). Furthermore, rapid diagnoses and the individu-alisation of prescribed medicines promise major cost reductions, which are wel-comed by health administrators. According to a BCC Market Research report, the value of the global market for personalised medicine technology was projected to equal 14.4 billion US dollars in 2009 and was expected to more than double over a 5-year period to reach 29.2 billion US dollars in 2014 (BCC Market Research 2009). Within this overall projection, it was noted that "pharmacogenomics is a major revenue generating market" and constituted 4.1 billion dollars of the total personalised medicine market in 2009 and that this segment would likely reach a market value of 9.5 billion US dollars in 2014. The next largest market segment is the PoC market, whose value was 2.7 billion US dollars in 2009 and is expected to increase to 9.5 billion dollars by 2014. Other segments that are mentioned include pharmaceutical proteomic technologies, pharmacokinetics, pharmacogenetics, pharmacodynamics, stem cell therapy and metabolomics.

Patient organisations seek more effective treatments of diseases that are associ-ated with specific genetic characteristics (biomarkers) as a means of more dura-ble wellness because research, for example, enables the development of medicines that are effective for a relatively small proportion of patients. In other words, a further driving force is ideational and relates to pharmacogenetics (genomics, pro-teomics and other "-omics") as a powerful technoscientific imaginary envision-ing possible health futures (Jasanoff and Kim 2009; Jasanoff 2011). With these changes, perceptions of disease, ontologies and epistemologies are evolving as well, as is also likely (with considerable lag) for the underpinning structures of institutional arrangements and professions that are concerned with or directly involved in healthcare.

Molecular diagnostic technologies challenge a healthcare and financial system that has long depended on visible symptoms and gross clinical classification. As diseases are (re-)classified into distinct molecular subcategories, there will be pressure to shift from traditional pharmaceutical business economic models that focus on "one-size-fits-all" drugs (Paci and Ibarreta 2009).

PoC medicine is a concept that has emerged in the literature to encompass techniques for making the correct diagnosis and beginning the appropriate treatment immediately during the first contact with a patient. Personalised medicine is the concept of customising an optimum treatment based on detailed and specific genetic information pertaining to a patient and tailoring medication to individual needs. Both the concepts and practices that they entail are accompanied by a variety of evidence-related questions. These questions must be addressed successively as pharmacogenetic tests become available so that the crucial link to personalised medicine can be provided. The process of identifying patients who are most likely to respond to a particular drug requires the (a) identification, (b) development and (c) validation of "biomarkers" for diabetes, heart disease, cancer and other illnesses. The technologies necessary for development and marketing will also meet several institutional "hurdles" before they can be adopted into mainstream medicine: regulation; reimbursement; physician education; and ethical, legal and societal concerns (European Commission 2007; Martin et al. 2006; Royal Society 2005).

PoC testing accounts for approximately one-third of the global in vitro diagnostics (IVD) market (BCC Market Research 2009). Rapid tests at the PoC by healthcare professionals or by patients in their own homes are revolutionising the diagnostic sector. Driven by the necessity of earlier, accurate diagnostic information in guiding critical clinical decisions, technology advances, including miniaturisation, are enhancing the role of diagnostic tests in healthcare systems. Products that are used in diabetes care constitute the largest segment of the PoC market. Other important segments relate to conditions such as urinary tract infections, tuberculosis, and heart failure; early distant warnings for stroke; and bladder cancer tests.

Home use tests for HIV underline the need for quality control, insurance and prevention of the misuse of such tests. Insurance companies are also making progress in the personalised medicine market. Apart from demonstrating safety and quality, testing devices must be user friendly. These devices must be convenient and simple to use while also meeting the connectivity requirements of healthcare systems.

Some studies predict a future in which new technologies will replace the traditional reliance of physicians on their senses, which include vision, hearing and touch. Molecular diagnostics require genetic literacy, and the genetic approach assists in the enhancement of doctors' "senses" while customising treatments and prevention strategies for individual patients (Pai 2009). Furthermore, as diagnosing illnesses and monitoring patient conditions become increasingly automated and technologised, self-managed diagnostic devices place this aspect of the process in the hands of patients. Because the era of personalised medicine will evidently affect millions of people, this new type of medicine is also expected to change the perception and management of disease.

Thus, emerging health technologies, such as PPPM, not only engender grand visions but also reveal multiple possibilities and future problems whose existence depends on who is responsible and whose aims will be preferred. In addition to the combined pressures of market forces and new technologies, multiple actors, such as patient organisations, health workers at care institutions, and health administrators who want to reduce costs at the PoC in clinics, are important drivers of these developments (Martin et al. 2006; Paci and Ibarreta 2009).

Generally, the various actors who are involved have different perspectives, with pharmaceutical companies accenting potential market gains, health administrators favouring speed and efficiency in diagnostic regimens and patients and health workers in the field emphasising the validation and safety of treatments.[9] In other words, essential tensions may exist between those actors who primarily emphasise economic worth and technological efficacy and actors who place a premium on caring and view personalised medicine in terms of enabling social relations at the interface between health workers and physicians. Therefore, analyses of the interactions between value hierarchies at the institutional and personal levels are relevant to any inquiry regarding the role of new technologies as mediators between patients and those who diagnose and treat them or monitor their treatment.[10] This relevance also extends to the role of health workers with regard to the self-diagnostic capacity of patients in terms of their use of off-the-shelf diagnostic instruments on the market.

Attending to issues of knowledge production and transfer will ultimately recall the configuration of persons/patients (that is, issues of identity, politics and governance). One major barrier that health economics must consider is access to the health system, which is not necessarily equal for all potential users of healthcare and preventive medicine services for several reasons.

Another dimension that is highlighted in the policy literature is the significance of management methods and the shift from public to private-sector approaches, such as the new public management approach (Vedung 2010). Here, one finds arguments that the emphasis on competitiveness, the creation of quasi-markets in the healthcare sector and new audit cultures may have effects at the macro level (Lane 2000), and in turn, change processes at the micro and meso levels of governance and systems for patient self-regulation (van Essen 2005, 2009).

---

[9] This analysis is simplified due to matters of space and clarity of argument. To take the most explicit example, even if pharmaceutical companies must produce revenues for their owners, it is no easy task, with millions in developing expenditures and the always present possibility that new products will fail in one manner or another (Bragesjö and Hallberg 2011). It has even been suggested that the problem in the pharmaceutical sector is so severe that political actions are needed to support the industry, such as lower taxation or the requirement of pre-written contracts between healthcare providers and a company for the use of a technology under development.

[10] For a discussion of various value categories, or "worth", see Thevenot 2009; Zuiderent-Jerak 2007, 2009.

5.3 Expertise Among Evidence, Persons and Affordance

We are now in a position to return to the beginning of the chapter, and the assertions of PPPM will serve as a bridge between two significant and sometimes divergent movements within the healthcare system: evidence-based medicine and person-centred care.[11] By drawing on genetic knowledge fitted to each individual patient—rather than the average measures of large-population health benefits taken from randomised clinical trials or cohort studies—PPPM might ease conflict between evidence and persons (i.e., between allegedly hard science and soft humans).

In recent years, the term "evidence-based medicine" has been a catchword for profound changes in medical research and the provision of healthcare across the Western world. At the core of this concept, which was introduced in Canada in the early 1990s, is the idea that clinical decisions should be based on the most reliable knowledge available regarding the effects of medical interventions. Initiatives in the healthcare sector and numerous other areas are frequently justified by referring to this idea. Methods and tools that have been canonized under the banner of evidence-based medicine, such as randomised clinical trials, systematic reviews and practice guidelines, have been introduced in the fields of social work, education, psychotherapy and criminal justice. However, the application of these tools in healthcare systems and elsewhere has proved significantly more complicated than was initially anticipated by proponents of evidence-based practice.

> Another recent trend is a shift from patient-centred to person-centred medicine, which is reflected, for example, in the coordinated global effort evident at a major conference in Geneva in May 2008 and, since then, in its annual follow-up conferences, as well as a new journal. The International Journal of Person Centered Medicine strives to move away from the utilitarian application of methodologically limited, biostatistically dominated studies that are conducted in epidemiological subpopulations toward a more humanistic model of care that is based on science and humanity for individuals who collectively constitute the social communities in which they are born and in which they will later die. (Miles and Mezzich 2011, p. 2).

The conference and the journal benefit from the broad-ranging participation of physicians, researchers, patient organisation representatives, social workers and other practitioners and are expected to further consolidate efforts and facilitate the development of research agendas and clinical capacity building in the same spirit (Mezzich and Miles 2011).

Clearly, the ability to bridge these two major trends within medicine is a strategic asset, if realisable. Rather than discussing how real or imagined this promise of PPPM is, at present, it is necessary to discuss this discursive space in which PPPM allegedly fits like a glove. Evidence-based medicine and person-centred care are often placed along a spectrum of trust; a greater or lesser amount of confidence may be ascribed to humans and their competences and concerns compared with technologies, standards and the removal of personal subjective elements. The spectrum has a long history, although this history appears in many guises, such

---

[11] Please note the difference between "person-centred" and "personalised" medicine/care.

as the oppositions between idiographic and nomothetic research, hermeneutics and positivism, and qualitative and quantitative studies. However, many deeply involved actors, whether they are representatives of evidence-based medicine or person-centred care, are nuanced and do not rely entirely on technologies or personal competences, respectively. However, the opposition between persons and evidence is recurring and is thus a fundamental tension in the field. This conflict contributes heavily to the space in which the discursive roles of all of these movements, including PPPM, are determined.

This discussion provides preliminary information regarding the analyses of medicine and emerging health technologies: analyses that are based on this dichotomy may reinforce existing conflicts and thus support evidence or patients. Within multidisciplinary studies of science, technology and medicine, there have been many attempts to shift perspectives from focuses on nature versus society, humans versus nonhumans, and quantitative versus qualitative character and instead explore how technologies are constructed. Among these attempts are post-humanist approaches, such as actor-network theory, which has allocated agency symmetrically (that is, both to humans and technologies and other material, "non-human" entities). The purpose has been to examine how technologies are endowed with capacities and the various roles within medicine, for instance. Rather than discussing the opposition of technologies and people, such approaches focus on "hybrids" and the work that these hybrids perform. PPPM could be approached through such symmetrical, post-humanist methods. Through detailed studies of PPPM in action, this type of analysis could reveal how hybrids, such as pharmacogenomics and e-health/e-care, are constructed in laboratories and shifted from universities and companies to healthcare providers and patients, resulting in transformative effects for many of the involved persons.

We are inspired by these approaches. It is critical to avoid demonising or idealising either humans or technologies. It is also crucial to empirically acknowledge the plethora of hybrids and the many combinations of non-human technological solutions and human skills and values. Attending to hybrids may constitute a passable path that is certainly supported by the impressive number of detailed and informative case studies that draw on these notions. However, from the perspective of this chapter, one important reservation is connected to the particularities of the field of medicine and the ambition to overcome dichotomies: actors themselves are already at work analysing the field in these terms.

In particular, proponents of PPPM draw on the polarisation as a strategic asset when presenting PPPM as a technologically mediated solution to the dichotomy between evidence and persons. We fear that the pursuit of a post-humanist symmetry between technologies and people or between evidence and persons risks succumbing to the hype related to and the fascination with emerging technologies; this hype may be the greatest enemy of these emerging technologies. We will emphasise that there is nothing theoretically wrong with the symmetrical study of hybrids. However, the context of analysis is excessively tense because the actors themselves are greatly interested in the power of hybrids. Therefore, we suggest an "ontological fold": a slight asymmetry in the otherwise necessary focus on hybrids and the construction of technologies.

Thus, we argue that post-humanist approaches lack an analytical space for expertise and a clear role for humans and their collective tacit knowledge. The fundamental distinction, or "human bias", cannot be disregarded because it affects empirical analyses on several levels; this bias essentially assumes that all knowledge is primarily a matter of collective tacit knowledge that is developed and possessed communally among people. Much or most of this knowledge can be made explicit in formulas, machines and routines and publicly scrutinised through systematic investigations. In situations in which this ontological fold is overlooked either in practice or in theory, the result is excessive trust in the formulas, machines and routines that result from knowledge that was originally collective and tacit.

We claim that this result would occur with respect to PPPM if expertise is not placed at the centre of analysis. In this broader context, we need to find an analytic framework for issues concerning emerging health technologies that focuses on expertise rather than evidence—without idealising humans on behalf of technologies. Nuances are crucial. We are aware that such an attempt is a discursive minefield. The framework cannot and will not collapse into a Habermasian call against the technification of the patients' life-worlds mentioned above because this presupposes a dichotomy between technology and people. Rather, we are inspired by Carl May's focus on technology, patients and doctors and regard this focus as crucial to avoiding some of the pitfalls of extremist faith in evidence. Evidence always requires people. Regardless of how high-tech any health system becomes, such systems are created and used by people who are affected by such systems in their mundane daily lives. Knowledge presupposes and affects humans. Expertise is a term that refers to this essentially human element, which we believe to be crucial when studying possible enhancements of high-tech developments within the field of health and medicine.

Given the above position and arguments, how can this be turned into studies that take this into account? Below, we offer a framework that we believe will go some way towards addressing these problems. The framework is illustrated with Nelly Oudshoorn's interesting case study of telemedicine focusing mostly on the implementation and use of three telecare devices in the Netherlands and in Germany (Oudshoorn 2011, 2012). Oudshoorn's "multi-site" study was pursued independently of our framework and is presented most extensively in her book Telecare Technologies and the Transformation of Healthcare (2011).

5.4 Future Studies of Emerging Health Technologies: Concepts and a Framework

Considering the polarisation between evidence and persons, if we are to follow May, the next step is to monitor the transformative effects of materiality (that is, what the post-humanist approaches, such as recent Actor-Network Theory (ANT), have examined). Technologies—whether digital decision support, pharmacogenomics or e-health—afford new ways for expertise to travel, and thereby, reconfigure human relations. Expertise has an essentially human aspect, but this aspect interacts with and is altered by materiality in unpredictable ways. Thus, the three key elements of our analytical approach are in place: the affordance of technology, the travelling of expertise and the governance of expertise.

First, a pre-condition for telemedicine and pharmacogenomics, if not all technologies, is that some elements of expertise (some of which are allegedly tacit) can travel through and with non-human artefacts. In fact, expertise can travel. This ability to travel is clearly inherent in PPPM as an element of the concepts of telemedicine, e-health and pharmacogenomics and is exemplified in PoC diagnostics. PPPM exists as expertise that travels through healthcare systems from medical companies, state authorities, expert bodies and patient organisations to individual treatment decisions made among doctors, clinical teams and patients. Some elements of expertise are easily moveable, whereas other elements are ultimately not. Which elements are moveable and which elements are not? The answer to this question is crucial in understanding the fascination with emerging health technologies.

A second, equally important element involves how movements occur and in what direction they occur. Various material cultures are utilised when expertise travels. Different materialities offer different sets of possibilities and limitations. Technological devices or genetic microarrays may be used to enhance the interaction between the healthcare system and patients, or guidelines, protocols, algorithms or even organisational forms, such as formal or informal networks, should perhaps conduct these duties. According to our introduction of the concept, different materialities afford rather than determine the interaction between technologies and users.

These possibilities may be stated but must be further examined. How do various materialities, usually technologies, afford further paths of action? That technologies limit future paths is well known, but it may be hypothesised that a growing market in pharmacogenomics will sometimes limit paths more than necessary for reasons of profit. Simplification and standardisation are often profitable pursuits. However, the opposite is also true. Limitations may require enforcement to protect personal integrity, as the corporate sector (e.g., insurance companies) may identify opportunities for maximising profits by "marking" people genetically, as envisioned by Pálsson (2002), Evelyn Fox Keller (2000) and others. By attending to the affordance of technologies, analysts will be able to contribute to alternative reconfigurations by revealing cracks in the black boxes of PPPM as they are stabilised.

Third, the reason for the importance of the travelling expertise and affordance of technologies in studies of PPPM involves the relationships at stake. Who is deemed an expert? Who is allowed to influence the configurations within PPPM? Technologies afford different relationships between actors in the healthcare systems; for example, patients are empowered and/or disempowered, or doctors' autonomy is confirmed and/or constrained in various and new ways. Many actors battle for influence. On one level, these issues are overtly democratic and relevant for all interested parties and are clearly important for analysis and deliberation.

The manner in which the travelling and packaging of expertise often result in initially opaque consequences for patients, physicians and other involved parties is likely to be even more interesting for future empirical studies of emerging health technologies. Thus, the travelling of expertise and the affordance of technologies can be understood as various forms of governance, which is a composite of the materialities that are involved when knowledge is produced and initiated through healthcare systems. Of course, post facto stabilisations may be difficult to unravel or undo but remain important. In this sense, the governance of expertise is a critical issue for future studies of emerging health technologies.

5.4.1 Future Studies of Emerging Health Technologies: An Illustration

Rather than concluding on a mere conceptual level, we will end this chapter by applying our framework to a case study of telemedicine. We did not conduct this study; rather, we have borrowed it from Nelly Oudshoorn's recent work to make our own argument. The case study will illustrate the analytical objective of the three-layered framework.

Oudshoorn (2011) has written an excellent book in which many of the expectations in telemedicine are discussed and confronted empirically. She has interviewed patients and professionals about the actual workings of existing telecare technologies, such as mobile electrocardiogram (ECG) recorders and home monitors for heart failure. She notices the common vision in telecare: the vision of overcoming distance and thereby rendering outpatient clinics redundant. Here is her retelling of the experiences of a Mr X diagnosed with heart failure:

> The heart-failure nurse explained that he should use a wireless scale and blood-pressure meter daily. He thought it was a kind of magic because these instruments would send his measurements automatically to the telemedical centre, where a telenurse would control them. But since this conversation he feels rather tense. Why is he no longer allowed to visit the heart-failure nurse? She was such a kind lady and she took good care of him. And what about these instruments? He did not dare to tell the nurse, but he does not feel at ease with all the new electronic equipment in use nowadays. Why should he take his blood pressure himself? Why couldn't the nurse do it, as she always used to do? (Oudshoorn 2011, pp. 3–4).

This particular patient did not enrol in the offered telemedical program; no scale or blood-pressure meter was placed in his home. One major and common objection expressed by patients who declined enrolment was that they did not wish to transform their homes into clinics. In one case, Oudshoorn shows how weight and blood pressure monitors become visible, audible and permanent guests of the patient's home, occupying physical and mental space. People's homes have been the focus of seminal geographical work on telemedicine that Oudshoorn purposely invokes (Cartwright 2000). Geography indicates the importance of place. Places are not neutral but are influenced by technologies and, in turn, influence people's identities. Oudshoorn calls for "technogeographical" studies of care to capture these spatial aspects of telemedicine.

When following the movements of things and people between hospitals and homes, Oudshoorn finds what Paul Edwards refers to as various forms of "frictions", that is, resistances, costs and losses when data are gathered, computed, shared and moved. According to Edwards, there are no frictionless movements (Edwards 2010; Edwards et al. 2011). Oudshoorn (2012, p. 122) claims that although literal networks are often involved in telemedicine, "the erasure of distance" or "a free flow of information and people" does not result. We call for the study of travelling expertise in the vein of geography and frictions. Expertise is not moved without frictions, despite networks and black boxes. Expertise travels within geographies that pose their own constraints on the content and shapes of expertise.

It may be possible to move expertise in heart-failure into patients' homes, but these movements come at a cost. Costs and frictions, as well as new possibilities, are tied to the affordances of the technologies in use (Tweed 2010). Some things are enabled and allowed. Other things are not. The technological appliances promised to Mr X can speak, flash lights and display graphs. These appliances can send information themselves to the telemedical centre. The wireless scale that talks invites the interest of younger relatives visiting one patient's home. Graphs displayed on the TV facilitate the participation of patients' partners in caring for the patient and may also impress visiting friends. Oudshoorn finds that the blood pressure meter must be integrated into and thus transform the morning routines of both patients and their partners. However, for Mr X, the key loss introduced by the promised appliances is the skill and kindness of the nurse. These attributes are difficult to convey through the technologies but not always impossible. One example of possibilities in this area is the use of the communication program Skype between grandparents and grandchildren or between spouses who are separated for a period of time. By focusing on affordance, the view of technologies as "open-ended" is maintained without claims of limitless uses.

In another study, Oudshoorn (2012) describes how a mobile ECG monitor is used. The purpose of the monitor is to enable measurement of the heart rhythm both at home and in public places. Unfortunately, the device is designed to emit a very indiscrete sound. Because of this irritating sound, it is difficult to maintain privacy when using the device in public. The ECG monitor is designed to allow measurement in public, but, in fact, resists such use among many users because of its audible affordance. This affordance is not intrinsic, but rather, is a matter of packaging. The device could be differently designed but has not been.

> In principle, the problems patients faced with the recorder's sound script could have been solved with small changes in the artefact. Using light or vibration instead of sound as feedback could have been an appropriate solution, but the producer of the ambulatory recorder did not offer this option (interview, Jurgens, 16 December 2004). The responsibility to solve these problems were delegated to the patients, who had to put effort into "repairing" the technological script. (Oudshoorn 2012, p. 135).

Affordance is not ultimate definitive and can be changed. However, it may be more difficult to convey feelings and care than to change the sounds made by an ECG monitor.

Travelling of expertise and affordance of technologies are interesting in themselves but are not the primary focus of our approach. Most interesting in our view is the effects on responsibilities and the shifting relationship between patients/users and experts/physicians/professionals, that is, the issues of governance. In Oudshoorn's cases, these consequences are very clear. She devotes the last part of her book to the resulting redefinitions of patients. These redefinitions include not only patients but also their kin.

> It frequently happened that the partner, who was often present during our visit, joined in the conversation and told us very interesting things that we would not have noticed had we focused exclusively on the person expected to use the device. The telecare device thus redefines social relations in the home beyond the individual patient. (Oudshoorn 2012, p. 131).

The domestic relationships are transformed through the telemedical appliances. When studying technologies, the restructuring of relationships and identities is visible everywhere. According to Oudshoorn's observations, patients become lay experts or semi-professionals:

> The introduction of telecare technologies into the home thus transforms patients into 'assistant medical personnel', who actively participate in monitoring their own bodies (Oudshoorn 2012, p. 131).

We claim that this aspect of governance is crucial. Oudshoorn does not make this aspect as visible as it should be, as she lacks a clear vocabulary and a focus on issues of governance. On this issue we are heavily inspired by Carl May and his colleagues who explicitly draw on the body of literature on governance when studying the effects of telemedicine on patient identities:

> Telehealthcare may facilitate meetings between professionals but, in so doing, do these systems also end up leaving patients out of the loop? If so, how can patients reemerge into the consultation in any meaningful way? As certain roles are inscribed and prescribed for patients, so the opportunities for opening up the governance of this sociotechnical reshaping of health care provision are, we argue, constricted. (Mort et al. 2009, p. 12).

In order to open up the technogovernance exercised through telehealthcare these authors enter into close interaction with citizens through a pilot panel where the ramifications and future configurations of medicine at a distance are directly dealt with. This is one important added value of a focus on the governance of expertise. Equally important is the connection between these mundane consequences of technologies and the economic and structural changes driving these developments. The first quote provided about Mr X from Oudshoorn's book concludes by clarifying that whether he decides to accept the equipment now, he will finally be forced to do so. At least, this is the result for which this particular health insurer in the Netherlands hopes.

> He wonders what he should do and phones his health insurer who runs the telemedical centre. He is told that in the near future he has to use their new health service because they will no longer reimburse his visits to the heart-failure policlinic. End of story, he thought. (Oudshoorn 2011, pp. 3–4).

By focusing on the governance of expertise the questions will be who attempts to decide what for whom. When reading Oudshoorn, we observe a glimpse of this aspect of governance, but this aspect is not elaborated upon. She uses the quote to display the importance of her study but does not continue down the path of the combination of multiple stakeholders in the transition to telemedicine.

By briefly re-analysing Oudshoorn's case, we have presented a few instances in which the case study could have been enriched by using our three-layered framework. In future studies on emerging health technologies it will be key to draw on existing work on governance and combine it with the travelling of expertise and the affordance of technologies. By simultaneously studying these three aspects, we hope to find new connections. Without attending to the affordance of technologies and the travelling of expertise, studies of governance easily will lack nuances; without an eye on the issues of governance, studies of affordance of technologies and travelling of expertise are not blind but have impaired vision. We acknowledge that work, to be completed by ourselves and others, toward the combination of these elements, remains.

5.5 Concluding Remarks: Possible Re-conceptualisation?

When addressing the central questions regarding physician-patient interplay and the role of medical expertise anew, we suggest a special focus on the movements, practices and technologies of medical knowledge and the resulting emerging mutualities among actors. These aspects of medical knowledge can be and have been analysed in many ways, but here, we have suggested a specific combination of three analytical lenses. In the framework presented, we stress the prominence of expertise over materiality. In relation to post-humanist symmetry among technologies, things, evidence and people, the framework hence introduces a slight asymmetry (although there is nothing theoretically or principally wrong with symmetry). However, in studies of the affordance of emerging health technologies and governance, we need to create a clear space for human expertise and collective tacit knowledge. Without this space, we risk an unnecessary trust in pure formulas, machines and routines, for which expertise are vital every step of the way to ensuring that technologies and knowledge travel as intended.

First, medical knowledge exists as expertise that travels through healthcare systems from medical companies, state authorities, expert bodies and patient organisations to individual treatment decisions made among doctors, clinical teams and patients. Second, various material cultures are utilised when expertise travels. Perhaps technological devices or genetic microarrays are supposed to enhance the interaction between the healthcare system and patients, or perhaps guidelines, protocols, algorithms or even organisational forms, such as formal or informal networks, should conduct these duties. Different materialities afford different relationships between actors in the healthcare systems; for example, patients may be empowered or disempowered, and the autonomy of doctors may be confirmed or constrained. Third, the travelling and affordance of expertise can be understood as various forms of governance, which constitute a composite of the materialities that are involved when knowledge is produced and initiated through healthcare systems. We believe that using this heuristic scheme to identify ideal typical patterns or configurations for the purposes of conducting comparative analyses across disease categories and governance approaches in different European countries may be both interesting and policy-relevant.

Acknowledgments This research is supported by grants from The Swedish Research Council (2005-2373 and 2007-1633). We are also deeply in debt for the continuous support from Kristian Wasen.

References

Barrett, B. J. (2005). *Patient self-management tools: An overview*. Oakland: California Healthcare Foundation. Available http://www.chcf.org/publications/2005/06/patient-selfman-agement-tools-an-overview. Accessed 18 March 2012.

BCC Market Research. (2009). *Personalized medicine: Technologies and the global market report PHM044B*. (Press Release).

Bergen, D., Hutchinson, K., Nolan, J. T., & Weber, D. (2010). Effects of infant-parent play with a technology-enhanced toy: Affordance-related actions and communicative interactions. *Journal of Research in Childhood Education, 24*, 1–17.

Bird, A. (2011). What can philosophy tell us about evidence-based medicine? An assessment of Jeremy Howick's the philosophy of evidence-based medicine. *International Journal of Person Centered Medicine, 1*, 642–648.

Bloomfield, B. P., Latham, Y., & Vurdubakis, T. (2010). Bodies, technologies and action possibilities when is an affordance? *Sociology-the Journal of the British Sociological Association, 44*, 415–433.

Bloor, D. (1999a). Anti-latour. *Studies in History and Philosophy of Science, 30*, 81–112.

Bloor, D. (1999b). Reply to Bruno latour. *Studies in History and Philosophy of Science, 30*, 131–136.

Boden, M. A. (1996). *The philosophy of artificial life*. Oxford: Oxford University Press.

Bohlin, I., & Sager, M. (2011). *Evidensens många ansikten: evidensbaserad praktik i praktiken [The many faces of evidence: evidence-based practice in practice]*. Lund: Arkiv Förlag.

Bourret, P. (2005). BRCA patients and clinical collectives: New configurations of action in cancer genetics practices. *Social Studies of Science, 35*, 41–68.

Bragesjö, F., & Hallberg, M. (2011). Dilemmas of a vitalizing vaccine market: Lessons from the MMR vaccine/autism debate. *Science in Context, 24*, 107–125.

Brown, N., & Webster, A. (2004). *New medical technologies and society*. Cambridge: Polity Press.

Callon, M., & Latour, B. (1992). Don't throw the baby out with the bath school! A reply to collins and yearley. In A. Pickering (Ed.), *Science as practice and culture* (pp. 343–368). Chicago: University of Chicago Press.

Camacho, N., Landsman, V., & Stremersch, S. (2009). The connected patient. In S. Wuyts, M. Dekimpe, E. Gijsbrechts, & R. Pieters (Eds.), *The connected customer: The changing nature of consumer and business markets*. London: Routledge.

Candlin, C. N. (2000). The Cardiff lecture 2000—reinventing the patient/client: New challenges to health care communication. *Health Communication*, http://www.cf.ac.uk/encap/resources/HCRC-candlinlecture.pdf. Accessed March 4, 2011.

Cartwright, L. (2000). Reach out and heal someone: Telemedicine and the globalization of health care. *Health, 4*, 347–377.

Chamberlain, J. M. (2010). Portfolio-based performance appraisal for doctors: A case of paperwork compliance. *Sociological Research Online, 15*. doi:10.5153/sro.2099

Chamberlain, J. M. (2011). Teaching and learning guide for: Regulating the medical profession: From club governance to stakeholder regulation. *Sociology Compass, 5*, 116–120.

Clarke, A. E., Shim, J. K., Mamo, L., & Shim, J. K. (2003). Biomedicalization: Technoscientific transformations of health, illness, and U.S Biomedicine. *American Sociological Review, 68*, 161–194.

Cole, D. (2009). The Chinese room argument. *The Stanford Encyclopedia of Philosophy*, September 22, 2009, http://plato.stanford.edu/entries/chinese-room/. Accessed April 4 2012.

Collins, H. M. (1992). *Changing order: Replication and inducation in scientific practice* (2nd ed.). Chicago: University of Chicago Press.

Collins, H. M. (2004). Interactional expertise. *Phenomenology and the Cognitive Sciences, 3*, 125–143.

Collins, H. M. (2007). Case studies of expertise and experience. *Studies in History and Philosophy of Science, 38*, 615–760.

Collins, H. (2009). We cannot live by scepticism alone. *Nature, 458*, 30–31.

Collins, H. M., & Evans, R. (2002). The third wave of science studies: Studies of expertise and experience. *Social Studies of Science, 32*, 235–296.

Collins, H. M., & Evans, R. (2007). *Rethinking expertise*. Chicago: University of Chicago Press.

Collins, H., & Kusch, M. (1998). *The shapes of actions: What humans and machines can do*. Cambridge MA: MIT Press.

Collins, H., & Yearley, S. (1992a). Epistemological chicken. In A. Pickering (Ed.), *Science as practice and culture* (pp. 321–326). Chicago: University of Chicago Press.

Collins, H., & Yearley, S. (1992b). Journey into space. In A. Pickering (Ed.), *Science as practice and culture*. Chicago: University of Chicago Press.

Collins, C. D., Purohit, S., Podolsky, R. H., Zhaoa, H. S., Schatzc, D., Eckenrodea, S. E., et al. (2006). The application of genomic and proteomic technologies in predictive, preventive and personalized medicine. *Vascular Pharmacology, 45*, 258–267.

Corburn, J. (2007). Community knowledge in environmental health science: co-producing policy expertise. *Environmental Science and Policy, 10*, 150–161.

Cornwall, A., & Shankland, A. (2008). Engaging citizens: Lessons from building Brazil's national health system. *Social Science and Medicine, 66*, 2173–2184.

Croft, P., Malmivaara, A., & van Tulder, M. (2011). The pros and cons of evidence-based medicine. *Spine (Phila Pa 1976), 36*, E1121–E1125.

Dreyfus, H. L., Dreyfus, S. E., & Athanasiou, T. (1986). *Mind over machine : The power of human intuition and expertise in the era of the computers*. New York: Free Pres.

Edwards, P. (2010). *A vast machine: Computer models, climate data, and the politics of global warming*. Cambridge MA: MIT Press.

Edwards, P. N., Mayernik, M. S., Batcheller, A. L., Bowker, G., & Borgman, C. (2011). Science friction: Data, metadata, and collaboration. *Social Studies of Science, 41*, 667–690.

European Commission. (2007). Opinion on the ethical aspects of nanomedicine—report by the European group on ethis in science and new technologies to the EC, Brussels.

Evans, R., & Collins, H. M. (2007). Expertise: From attribute to attribution and back again. In E. J. Hackett, O. Amsterdamska, M. Lynch, & J. Wajcman (Eds.), *Handbook of science and technology studies* (pp. 609–630). Cambridge, MA: MIT Press.

Ford-Eickhoff, K., Plowman, D. A., & McDaniel, R. R. (2011). Hospital boards and hospital strategic focus: The impact of board involvement in strategic decision making. *Health Care Management Review, 36*, 145–154.

Gibson, J. J. (1979). *The ecological approach to visual perception*. Boston: Houghton Mifflin.

Golubnitschaja, O. (2010). Time for new guidelines in advanced diabetes care: Paradigm change from delayed interventional approach to predictive, preventive & personalized medicine. *The EPMA Journal, 1*, 3–12.

Grankvist, H. (2011). *Making doable problems within controversial science: US and Swedish Scientists' experience of gene transfer research.* Dissertation, Linköping, Sweden: Linköpings University.

Hackett, E. J., Amsterdamska, O., Lynch, M., & Wajcman, J. (2007). *The handbook of science and technology studies* (3rd ed.). Cambridge, MA: MIT Press.

Hedgecoe, A. (2006). Pharmacogenetics as alien science: Alzheimer's disease, core sets and expectations. *Social Studies of Science, 36,* 723–752.

Hedgecoe, A., & Martin, P. (2003). The drugs don't work: Expectations and the shaping of pharmacogenetics. *Social Studies of Science, 33,* 327–364.

Hindmarsh, R., & Prainsack, B. (2010). *Genetic suspects: Global governance of forensic DNA profiling and databasing.* Cambridge: Cambridge University Press.

Holmes, D., Murray, S. J., Perron, A., & Rail, G. (2006). Deconstructing the evidence-based discourse in health sciences: truth, power and fascism. *International Journal of Evidence Based Healthcare, 4,* 180–186.

Jasanoff, S. (2004). *States of knowledge : the co-production of science and the social order,:* London: Routledge.

Jasanoff, S. (2011). *Reframing rights: Bioconstituionalism in the genetic age.* Cambridge, MA: MIT Press.

Jasanoff, S., & Kim, S. H. (2009). Containing the Atom: Sociotechnical imaginaries and nuclear power in the United States and South Korea. *Minerva, 47,* 119–146.

Johnson, E., & Berner, B. (2010). *Technology and medical practice : Blood, guts and machines.* Farnham: Ashgate.

Keller, E. F. (2000). *The century of the gene.* Cambridge, MA: Harvard University Press.

Kerr, A., Cunningham-Burley, S., & Tutton, R. (2007). Shifting subject positions—experts and lay people in public dialogue. *Social Studies of Science, 37,* 385–411.

Lane, J.-E. (2000). *New public management.* London: Routledge.

Latour, B. (1999). *Pandora's hope: Essays on the reality of science studies.* Cambridge, MA: Harvard University Press.

Leonardi, P. M. (2011). When flexible routines meet flexible technologies: Affordance, constraint, and the imbrication of human and material agencies. *MIS Quarterly, 35,* 147–167.

Lofgren, H., & de Boer, R. (2004). Pharmaceuticals in Australia: Developments in regulation and governance. *Social Science and Medicine, 58,* 2397–2407.

Marcant, O. (2008). Research in social sciences and needs in expertise in the public policies: The example of the protection of water resources. *ESSACHESS: Revue interdisciplinaire de sciences humaines et sociales* (pp. 169–178).

Martin, P., Lewis, G., Smart, A., & Webster, A. (2006). *False positive? The clinical and commercial development of pharmacogenetics.* York: SATSUUniversity of Nottingham, University of York and IGBIS.

May, C., Mort, M., Williams, T., & Gask, L. (2003). Health technology assessment in its local contexts: Studies of telehealthcare. *Social Science and Medicine, 57,* 697–710.

May, C., Rapley, T., Moreira, T., Finch, T., & Heaven, B. (2006). Technogovernance: Evidence, subjectivity, and the clinical encounter in primary care medicine. *Social Science and Medicine, 62,* 1022–1030.

Mezzich, J. E., & Miles, A. (2011). The third Geneva conference on person-centered medicine: Collaboration across specialties, disciplines and programs. *The International Journal of Person Centered Medicine, 1,* 6–9.

Mezzich, J. E., Snaedal, J., van Weel, C., Botbol, M., & Salloum, I. (2011). Introduction to person-centred medicine: from concepts to practice. *Journal of evaluation in clinical practice, 17,* 330–332.

Miles, A., & Mezzich, J. E. (2011). Advancing the global communication of scholarship and research for personalized healthcare. *International Journal of Person Centered Medicine, 1,* 2.

Milewa, T. (2006). Health technology adoption and the politics of governance in the UK. *Social Science and Medicine, 63,* 3102–3112.

Moore, A. (2010). Public bioethics and public engagement: the politics of "proper talk". *Public Understanding of Science, 19*, 197–211.

Mort, M., Finch, T., & May, C. (2009). Making and unmaking telepatients identity and governance in new health technologies. *Science, Technology and Human Values, 34*, 9–33.

Norman, D. A. (1988). *The psychology of everyday things*. New York: Basic Books.

Oh, H., Rizo, C., Enkin, M., & Jadad, O. (2005). What is eHealth (3): A systematic review of published definitions. *Journal of Medical Internet Research, 7*, e1. doi:10.2196/jmir.7.1.e1.

Oudshoorn, N. (2011). *Telecare technologies and the transformation of healthcare*. Basingstoke: Palgrave Macmillan.

Oudshoorn, N. (2012). How places matter: Telecare technologies and the changing spatial dimensions of healthcare. *Social Studies of Science, 42*, 121–142.

Paci, D., & Ibarreta, D. (2009). Economic and cost-effectiveness conditions for pharmacogenetics tests: An integral part of translational research and innovation uptake in personalized medicine. *Current Pharmacogenetics and Personalized Medicine, 7*, 284–296.

Pai, A. (2009). Genomic medicine in healthcare—the tip of the iceberg. *Electronic Healthcare, 8*, e1–e13.

Pálsson, G. (2002). Medical databases: The icelandic case. In S. Lundin & L. Åkesson (Eds.), *Gene technology and economy*. Lund: Nordic Academic Press.

Petersson, J. (2011). Medicine at a distance in Sweden: Spatiotemporal matters in accomplishing working telemedicine. *Science Studies, 24*, 43–63.

Pfaffenberger, B. (1992). Technological dramas. *Science, Technology and Human Values, 17*, 282–312.

Pickering, A. (1992). *Science as practice and culture*. Chicago: University of Chicago Press.

Royal Society (2005) *Personalised medicines: hopes and realities*. The Royal Society, September.

Runhaar, H. A. C., Van Der Sluijs, J. R., & Driessen, P. R. J. (2009). Shifts in environmental health risk governance: An analytical framework. *Safety, Reliability and Risk Analysis: Theory, Methods, and Applications—Proceedings of the Joint ESREL and SRA-Europe Conference* (p. 369).

Sager, M. (2006). *Pluripotent circulations: Putting actor-network theory to work on stem cells in the US 1998–2001*. Gothenburg: University of Gothenburg.

Salter, B., Gottweis, H., & Waldby, C. (2009). *The global politics of human embryonic stem cell science: Regenerative medicine in transitio*. Basinstoke: Palgrave.

Searle, J. (1980). Minds, brains, and programs. *Behavioral and Brain Sciences, 3*, 417–457.

Searle, J. R. (1999). *Mind, language and society: Doing philosophy in the real world*. London: Weidenfeld & Nicolson.

Selinger, E., & Crease, R. P. (2006). *The philosophy of expertise*. New York: Columbia University Press.

Singer, E. (2010). A vision for personalized medicine. *Technology Review*, http://www.technologyreview.com/biomedicine/24703/ Accessed March 9 2010.

Sismondo, S. (2004). *An introduction to science and technology studies*. Malden: Blackwell.

Sood, S., Mbarika, V., Jugoo, S., Dookhy, R., Doarn, C. R., Prakash, N., et al. (2007). What is telemedicine? A collection of 104 peer-reviewed perspectives and theoretical underpinnings. *Telemedicine Journal and E-Health, 13*, 573–590.

Stephanie, T. (2010). Comparing approaches towards governing scientific advisory bodies on food safety in the United States and the European union. *Wisconsin Law Review, 627*, 627–671.

Suchman, L. (2010). Moving nature/culture. In E. Johnson & B. Berner (Eds.), *Technology and medical practice : Blood, guts and machines* (pp. 203–208). Farnham: Ashgate.

Thevenot, L. (2009). Governing life by standards: A view from engagements. *Social Studies of Science, 39*, 793–813.

Torpy, J. M., Lynm, C., & Glass, R. M. (2009). JAMA patient page. Evidence-based medicine. *JAMA, 301*, 900.

Tweed, C. (2010). Exploring the affordances of telecare-related technologies in the home. In M. Schillmeier & M. Domènech (Eds.), *New technologies and emerging spaces of care*. Farnham: Ashgate.

van Essen, A. M. (2005). Theorising the political controversy on the emergence of new public management in Health care reforms. Conference paper given at *The Network for European Social Policy Analysis: The Governance of Social Policy in the new Europe*. April 1–2, 2005. University of Bath.

van Essen, A. M. (2009). *Seeking a balance?! The emergence of new public management in new hospital payment systems in Germany, the Netherlands and the United Kingdom*. Dissertation, Vrije Universiteit, Amsterdam.

Vedung, E. (2010). Four waves of evaluation. *Evaluation, 6*, 263–277.

Webster, A. (2006). *New technologies in health care: Challenge, change and innovation*. Gordonsville: Palgrave Macmillan.

Weimer, D. L. (2010). Stakeholder governance of organ transplantation: A desirable model for inducing evidence-based medicine? *Regulation and Governance, 4*, 281–302.

Wilkinson, K., Lowe, P., & Donaldson, A. (2010). Beyond policy networks: Policy framing and the politics of expertise in the 2001 foot and mouth disease crisis. *Public Administration, 88*, 331–345.

Willems, D. (2000). Managing one's body using self-management techniques: Practicing autonomy. *Theoretical Medicine and Bioethics, 21*, 23–38.

Woolgar, S. (1992). Some remarks about positionism: A reply to Collins and Yearley. In A. Pickering (Ed.), *Science as practice and culture* (pp. 327–342). Chicago: University of Chicago Press.

Yearley, S. (2005). *Making sense of science: Understanding the social study of science*. London: Sage.

Zuiderent-Jerak, T. (2007). *Standardizing healthcare practices. Experimental interventions in medicine and science and technology studies*, Dissertation, Erasmus University, Rotterdam.

Zuiderent-Jerak, T. (2009). Competition in the wild: Reconfiguring healthcare markets. *Social Studies of Science, 39*, 765–792.